MANCHESTER UNITED IN EUROPE

MANCHESTER UNITED

IN EUROPE

Roger Macdonald

Illustrations designed by Rod McLeod

PELHAM BOOKS

First published in Great Britain by
PELHAM BOOKS
26 Bloomsbury Street
London W.C.1
1968

7207 0235 6

Printed in Great Britain by
Northumberland Press Limited
Gateshead

CONTENTS

ILLUSTRATIONS

ACKNOWLEDGEMENTS

Special thanks are due to players and officials of Manchester United Football Club, who provided much valuable information. Jack Rollin, Editor of *Soccer Star*, Norman Fox and Barry Davies read the proofs and suggested improvements.

Rod McLeod provided cartoons, the jacket design and the layout of pictures. The task of collecting them was eased considerably by 'Will' Wilson and Ron Ahrens of *Syndication International*, who went out of their way to satisfy the most unreasonable demands. Early pictures of United in Europe came from the files of *The Times*, to whom I am grateful for permission to reproduce some outstanding pictures of the European Cup Final—most of which have not been published previously. The photographer was Harry Kerr.

1

Prelude: Old Trafford

It's our turn to be Manchester United. Whether as gawky kids with dirty knees in a play street, scrambling in the gutters, risking calumny with shots around the window sills; or as grown men who know better but don't care, swiping at a tin can rattling in Warwick Road, or volleying a peanut bag into the cricketers' Old Trafford of Barlow and Hornsby. For the moment we have the freedom of the sky, to play at being gods. We run with the flowing grace of Charlton, swaying in and out of lamp-posts, sneering at their green immobility; our climax is volcanic, a shot of eruptive force, searing into an invisible net. Unless, of course, someone else is Stepney, a mid-air meteor with octopus arms who catches, deflects and punches the bombardment of imagery with daring nonchalance. Then we must be best, be Best, a phantom figure on a tightrope of tricks, uncoiling and recoiling, suspending the pull of gravity for the ultimate dribble, the ultimate goal. But time presses, so we scurry together from Clayton, where United played long ago and where the stands once fell down, across the Ship Canal on Trafford Bridge, past rows of chimney stacks, fuzzy outlines in the heavy air. Today no bridges swing open for tall ships: only the revving, impatient traffic impedes us as it congeals desperately around the ground, cars looking for a nook and cranny. Smugly, we press on towards Old Trafford's beckoning pylons that sharpen the murky skyline of factory and Gothic tower; we run the grinding gauntlet of the turnstiles, and jostle into the Stretford End where the scarves stretch and flutter and the rattles chatter like defiant war-cries. We wait: and in the mind's eye there is one footballer to every square yard, each shooting United's winning goal. Then the dream dissolves as our gods drop back into the third dimension, a file of red and white pours out to prepare for battle, and a wave of anticipatory noise laps at both ends of the ground. Soon, in a moment of disarming magic, the ball speeds from man to man and United score: the signal for an explosion of sound, a pulsating, pent-up crescendo that dies away, at last, in a rumble of ecstasy.

The fence—it is to protect the fans *from* Nobby Stiles

2

Sir Matt Busby

Matthew Busby was born in a two-roomed pitman's cottage, one of thirty-two in the tiny village of Orbiston, Lanarkshire, in 1910. His father worked down the pit, went off to fight in the war to end wars in 1914, and was killed by a sniper in the Arras mud two winters later. His mother stoically raised the family, three daughters and Matthew, who was soon engrained enough in football to look after the equipment of Orbiston Celtic, with their inside-left called Alex James. For all that, Matt was bright enough at school to enter the higher grade and for his headmaster, keeping him on after fifteen, to see him as a teacher.

Matt's mother had other ideas; of emigrating to the United States, which to many was a sort of Eldorado where hunger and poverty could be dispelled for ever. But the Eldorado had a waiting list of at least six months, and the eighteen-year-old Busby had to take the only temporary job he could find, down the Orbiston Colliery —a job, he said later, 'I never wish to try my hand at again.'

The delay was enough to alter his destiny. While Busby the miner slogged away underground, Busby the footballer graduated on the surface from a youth team called Alpine Villa to the Junior club, Denny Hibernian.

Their secretary, Alex McNeill, recommended him to Jimmy McMullan (their previous export to Manchester City) after only six matches. McMullan got Busby a trial, a Central League game away to Burnley, which was enough for City's manager, Peter Hodge, to offer him in February, 1929, a weekly wage of £5 per week as a full-time professional. To Busby, paid £2 a week for sweat and toil below the pithead, the offer was irresistible. Mrs Busby abandoned her plans to emigrate, accepting his decision with misgivings.

For a long time it seemed she was right, for while Matt Busby made his first team debut against Middlesbrough on November 2, he spent most of the season playing—and playing badly—as an inside-forward for the reserves. Busby decided to leave Manchester and his lodgings for good, packed his bags, and was only talked out of going by his room mate, Bill McCloy, after a long argument into the small hours. Then he fell ill with pneumonia, and was frankly surprised when City persevered and retained him for a second summer. Busby recalled: 'My confidence so deserted me the moment I returned to duty in July that I actually dreaded the approach of each football season.'

Not that City were all that anxious to keep him: they had one serious inquiry, from their neighbours and poor relations, Manchester United, who had been relegated and come close to bankruptcy. The chief scout at Old Trafford, Louis Rocca, had a shoestring budget that scarcely stretched to any significant transfer fee. Told by his directors to 'buy any reasonable inside-forward that you can get cheaply', Rocca telephoned Hodge at Maine Road to inquire after Busby. Hodge replied: 'We are quite willing to sell; you can have Busby for £150.'

Rocca's reply was sad and slightly sardonic. 'We couldn't afford 150 shillings, never mind pounds.' Both he and United, as one of their programmes ruefully recalled later, thought Busby valued too highly: 'He was rather a poor inside-forward and United were not taking any chances.'

The indifferent inside-forward, however, became an outstanding wing-half—a position he played in almost by accident. One of City's triallists failed to turn up for a Northern Midweek League match, and the trainer, Alex Bell, stuck Busby in at right-half. 'For the first time since coming to England,' said Busby, 'I actually enjoyed a game of football.'

Hodge noticed his improvement, picked him at right-half for the reserves, then, a week later, as replacement for the injured Malcolm Barrass against Huddersfield in the Football League. He played so well that Barrass, even when fit, could not win his place back again. Busby went on to take part in two Cup finals in successive years for City, losing and winning, and was capped by Scotland against Wales in 1934. Strong and clever, Busby could switch the direction of play with startling finesse and dexterity. His right-footed passing was remarkably accurate over long distances; his left foot imparted an astonishing spin, that whipped the ball over full-backs' heads, sending away the wingers.

For all this success, Busby became desperately unhappy at Maine Road. A leg injury kept him out of football for more than a year and his wife, Jean, was frequently ill. He became convinced that only a complete change of surroundings would bring a change of fortune. So in March, 1936, he asked for a transfer, and Liverpool put in a successful bid of £7,000.

Busby's arrival on Merseyside coincided with that of a new manager, the effervescent George Kay from West Ham, who in three years pulled the club out of trouble. Apart from his contribution on the field, Matt played a curious role in the capture of the legendary Billy Liddell. During the close season he returned to Scotland to play golf regularly with his former City and International colleague, Alex Herd, who always had an eye for new talent. Herd aroused the interest of Hamilton Academicals' manager in a fifteen-year-old winger on the books of a Junior club, Lochgelly Violet. Hamilton, though, could not guarantee the security wanted by Liddell's parents, so when Herd told Busby of their failure, he put in a long-distance call to Kay at Liverpool and persuaded him to better the offer. Liverpool succeeded where Hamilton had failed, signing their most brilliant player of the immediate post-war period.

But Liddell and Liverpool were left behind when Busby was called up for the duration of the war. He became a physical training instructor on a troopship, running for miles around the decks before the soldiers were awake to keep himself fit. Then, after the invasion of Italy, he was put in charge of a special squad of footballers detailed to stage exhibition matches for the armed forces' entertainment. Joe Mercer, later Manchester City's manager, said of Matt that he 'first saw the steel in him and realised his leadership when playing in Italy in an Army side during the war. We had thought he was a kindly, easy-going fellow with a lot of ability as a right-half. Then some big-name players started getting above themselves and Matt quickly told them to toe the line like everyone else'.

It was in Italy, at Bari, that Busby first met Jimmy

Murphy, a Welshman who put fire into coaching, whether it was clumsy soldiers or deft Italian youths. His dedication held Busby spell-bound, they became firm friends, and Matt promised that Murphy would become his assistant as soon as he secured an appointment as manager in England. It was, as Busby said afterwards, 'My first and greatest signing for Manchester United.'

Busby's experience in Italy confirmed his feeling that he should manage where he had previously played. 'I was thirty-six, and though football had been good to me in pre-war days, I was not foolish enough to imagine that I could feed a wife and two children on memories.

'I suppose I could have continued playing for a year or two, but that would only have delayed the day when I should have to think of doing something else for my bread and butter.

'Before the war there were few outlets for soccer players when their careers ended. Oh yes, one might get a job as a licensee of a hotel, but there were not enough hotels for every ex-player. In any event, that wasn't my plan. I had started in football determined that I should stay in it.'

Liverpool wanted to retain Busby's services as a coach, and early in 1945 they offered him a five-year contract—which he accepted verbally. On February 15, however, Manchester United's directors had what proved, in retrospect, a momentous meeting. James Gibson, the chairman, reported that a Mr M. Busby had visited him (he omitted to mention that he had encouraged the visit), having learned of a 'post-war vacancy for team-manager'. He had had several offers of such engagements elsewhere (which Busby had, from Reading and Ayr United) 'but would prefer to accept a position in the Manchester area for family reasons'. Gibson said he was 'impressed with Busby's ideas and honesty of purpose', and his enthusiasm carried the board to a unanimous decision. Busby was appointed for a first period of five years from one month after his demobilisation—precisely, from October 22, 1945.

The club that Busby took over was in a sorry plight. The Old Trafford ground had been extensively damaged by bombs on the night of March 11, 1940, and remained in ruins. The dressing-rooms were derelict, there were no training facilities, the offices had been moved to the chairman's business premises, Cornbrook Cold Stores. Matches were played, and continued to be until August, 1949, on Manchester City's ground at Maine Road. Many of the players, Carey, Pearson, Morris and Mitten among them, were still in the Army; and with an overdraft of £15,000 there was little money for transfers. Almost the only one of significance was that of Jimmy Delaney, who Celtic, misguidedly believing his career to be at an end, sold for a paltry £4,000.

Delaney proved an instant success; and so did Busby's revolutionary methods, which had impressed Gibson at their brief interview. From the outset, Busby was determined to find both freedom and security under one roof. 'I had to make certain that, unlike other unfortunates, I did not join a club prepared to tolerate my presence for, perhaps a couple of seasons, before showing me the door. I wanted a club that would give an opportunity to a man willing to work really hard for success.'

Busby began, and has continued, as a team dictator. 'I made no bones about it,' he said in 1965. 'The team would have to be my responsibility alone. If I flopped, then they could fire me.

'That was twenty years ago, and during that time I have not met with any interference from the directors. I wouldn't have put up with it, and I haven't had to.'

Perhaps more important, Busby had retired while still young and fit enough to play: he had no intention of running United from some remote desk and swivel chair. 'From the start,' he recalls, 'I spent most of my time in tracksuit and plimsolls, knowing that this way I stood a much better chance of getting to know my players than I would have had wearing a pin-striped suit in my office.'

Nor was Busby's unfamiliar relationship with his players restricted to greater contact on the field. In spite of a famous career, he had seen at close hand the grimmer side of the game before the emancipation of the professional footballer. Busby 'learned a lesson in those days at Manchester City. As a youngster, I felt there was too much class distinction at Maine Road, too large a gap between the established first team players and the rest of the playing staff. Team spirit always suffered. Snobbery has no place in a happy club, and I like to treat everyone on our books with equal consideration.

'As a footballer I had suffered and seen other players suffer. I thought I could handle men differently. I not only demand respect from players—I give respect to them.'

Busby's iron fist in velvet glove, a combination of authority, sympathy and Scottish charm, brought the best out of the available talent. It was, literally, a confidence trick, blending perception and subtle psychology to inspire players to make the fullest use of their skills.

This was achieved, in practical terms, by supreme versatility—a heresy roundly condemned by British football until the harsh lessons given by Hungary. 'This line of reasoning,' said Busby, 'was shattered by my experience as a Manchester City player. In the forward-line I was completely out of my depth, but after switching to half-back my value to City was doubled, even trebled.'

Busby is often said, disparagingly, to have inherited the exciting team that beat Blackpool in the 1948 F.A. Cup final. But in fact he made seven changes, three of them positional, from the team he fielded in his first peace-time season. In particular Johnny Carey—whose appointment as captain was described by Busby as 'one of the wisest moves I ever made'—and John Aston were switched from inside-forward to full-back, where they became probably the best pair in Britain; Allenby Chilton, too, moved from wing-half to centre-half with such striking success that he was capped by England near the end of his career.

When it came to adapting players to circumstances, Busby seemed to hold the wand of a magician. Carey, a player of infinite skill, appeared for United in nine different positions; but there were others. In 1951, when the team seemed to have gone stale, Busby introduced a new pair of full-backs, McNulty on the right and Byrne on the left, moving Carey from right-back to right-half. As Rowley was injured, Aston, who had begun his career at inside-forward, took over at centre-forward and scored fifteen goals. When Rowley regained fitness he resumed at outside-left, forming such a remarkable partnership with Pearson that England chose them both against Scotland in April, 1952.

Because Arsenal were panting at their heels, Busby reversed his changes with even greater élan when he felt they had outlived their impact. Aston returned to left-back, Rowley to centre-forward, and Byrne to outside-left (his earlier position in the reserves), where he proceeded to score in each of United's remaining five matches. Arsenal were beaten 6-0 in devastating fashion at Old Trafford and United took the title.

Yet improvisation, however inspired, was no substitute for vigour. The need for new players was apparent early in the 1952-53 season, when the championship team was paired at the foot of the table with Manchester City by the middle of October. United beat Aston Villa in a terrible match that made up Busby's mind. The same evening he told the directors: 'Something must be done, and I'm going to do it. I must be drastic, and make big changes. Even if everyone calls me crazy. I intend making the move which is going to make or break Manchester United.' On the following Wednesday Busby fielded a team of young footballers, most of them teenagers, in a friendly at Kilmarnock. They played so well, winning 3-0, that he kept seven of them for a League match at Huddersfield. They were unbeaten for their next seven games, and a legend was born.

3

The Young Lions

The Busby Babes, an epitaph which maligned their stature and maturity, evolved painstakingly over a decade. Their embryonic existence can be traced back to 1947, when Jimmy Murphy, by now in charge of the Central League team, told Matt candidly: 'Although we've won the reserve championship, not one of these players is really good enough for the first team.'

Busby's response was to step up his recruitment of youth, an idea which had been in his mind since he took over at Old Trafford, until four teams of varying ages could be fielded every Saturday—the 'B', for boys of 15 to 16½; the 'A', 16½-17½; the Colts, 16½-18½; and the official third or 'A' team, 18½-20. The system was always the same. First United's team of eight scouts, led by Joe Armstrong and Louis Rocca, would look at young players, concentrating on those who had represented their city or county. If Busby, or Murphy or Bert Whalley, the club coach, thought them sufficiently promising, they were brought to Manchester for one or more trials. The final selection were signed on as soon as they left school at fifteen. They trained with the first team, received intensive coaching, and were housed in specially selected lodgings if their homes were outside Manchester.

Roger Byrne, a Mancunian by birth, was the first of the new discoveries to establish himself in the League team, at twenty-one. He had been an inside-forward in the Ryder Brow Boys Club (in company with the England cricketer, Brian Statham) when Whalley saw him and signed him as an amateur, back in 1948. Graduating to the reserves as a quick but far from irresistible outside-left, he found his best position in defence, at left-back, where England capped him on thirty-three occasions. Busby, nevertheless, saw Byrne as a winger, it was only after he asked for a transfer in August, 1952, and stayed on the list for four days that he won a chance to prove himself in defence.

Although short and slightly built for a full-back, Byrne's determination was formidable; he drove himself to the limits of endurance for his team. If, judged at the highest level, his tackling was suspect and his heading lamentable, he remained the supreme professional: his mistakes were so few and far between that they were glaringly apparent; and, even then, his powers of recovery staggered his opponents. Above all, Byrne was a highly intelligent footballer, well educated, quick to sum up an opponent and a situation. His gamesmanship might have brought a shudder to the purist; but there was never the hint of a bad foul. Busby appointed him captain in February 1954, and his leadership, in terms of temperament and dedication, was often inspired.

Jeff Whitefoot, from Stockport, made his first appearance at wing-half against Portsmouth on April 5, 1950, when he was only sixteen. He was soon good enough to play for England's Under-23 team against Italy Under-23, but not to keep a place in United's half-back line in the face of fierce competition from Blanchflower, Colman, Edwards and Jones.

Mark Jones, by a curious twist, to all intents and purposes discovered himself in an England Schoolboys trial at Old Trafford, when to Manchester United he was a complete unknown. Busby was impressed, Armstrong and Rocca went to see him play several times while he was at school in Barnsley, and as soon as he left, snapped him up for United. Jones remained loyal to the club for five years until Chilton vacated the centre-half position. Even then he was not left unchallenged for long. The margin between him and Jackie Blanchflower was almost indiscernible, possession being nine points of the law. For a time, therefore, Jones kept out Blanchflower; but when Jones was injured in an F.A. Cup-tie at Bournemouth in 1957, Blanchflower took his place so brilliantly that he stayed for the rest of the season.

Blanchflower, brother of Aston Villa and Tottenham's Danny, came to Old Trafford before Busby had seen him play at all, solely on the recommendation of United's Irish scout, Bob Harper. After two disastrous experiments as an apprentice accountant and plumber, he became a full-time professional, yet at inside-forward still lacked the pace for First Division football. Busby solved the problem by switching him to centre-half, where he became an automatic choice for Northern Ireland, though still in United's reserves. While Jones was brawny, relentless, quite implacable, Blanchflower was less physical, but infinitely more flexible and adaptable to the moment. Only the supreme loyalty commanded at Old Trafford could have kept them both, at one club.

Blanchflower had a brief taste of first-team football in 1952, as did Bill Foulkes, destined to span two great teams in a single decade. Foulkes came from Thalto Heath, near St Helens, in the midst of the Lancashire coalfield. His father was a miner and the goalkeeper of New Brighton, then a flourishing club in the old Third Division North. Bill played football at Whiston Grammar School, but had no serious thoughts of it as a career, and eventually went into the pit at St Helens. Early in 1946 Whalley signed him on amateur forms, and after a few ups and downs, Foulkes got into the League side in December, 1952, facing Liverpool and the formidable Liddell. He played only one more game that season, but became United's regular right-back during the next.

Busby had a hard task persuading Foulkes to become a full-time professional. 'After all,' said Foulkes, who was a logical fellow when it came to brass, 'I was earning far more from mining than I did at Old Trafford. As an assistant to the under-manager at the colliery, I was getting £15 a week, which was a good wage for a young bloke in those days. When I first became a part-timer with United, I was paid £6 during the summer and £7 during the season. Now I knew that Chilton, the centre-half, was drawing £17 full-time—so what had I got to gain?'

If nothing else, a more tolerable existence. Foulkes must be the only professional to play for England when he was working down a pit from 7 a.m. to 2.30 p.m., catching the 3.45 train from St Helens, training at Manchester, taking the 9.15 train home and getting to bed exhausted about 11 p.m. Foulkes was chosen for one international, against Northern Ireland in 1955, and is bitter about losing his place. 'It was rather ridiculous,' he pointed out, 'for the England selectors to choose me after twenty-seven League games, then throw me on the scrapheap—and replace me with Staniforth of Huddersfield, who was already in his early thirties.'

Another son of a miner, David Pegg, also won one cap for England—in May, 1957, nine months before Munich. A Doncaster schoolboy, he was watched many times by a United scout, Norman Scholes, but after his outstanding performances for England Schools it was clear that there would be a queue for his signature. Birmingham were the favourites, but Busby's refusal to make extravagant promises impressed Pegg's father, who encouraged the boy to join Manchester United. However even as a full international Pegg was never sure of keeping out Albert Scanlon, an elusive winger with a fierce shot, born in Manchester and determined to establish himself in the United team.

Pegg played his first senior game against Middlesbrough in the 1952-53 season: so did another of the young lions, Duncan Edwards. Chosen at wing-half against Cardiff City on Easter Monday, April 4, 1953, at fifteen years and 285 days, Edwards was the youngest professional to play in First Division football.

One year, when Busby gave his usual informal talk to new or potential recruits, he noticed a big boy in the corner of the room whose eyes never left him, taking in every word. The boy was Edwards, already supreme in his own sphere, captain of the England Schoolboys side.

Edwards came from Dudley, Staffordshire, but Busby had little difficulty in stealing him from under the Wolves' noses. For Edwards had a passion to play for Manchester United, whom he thought the greatest club in the world. He said to a delighted Busby: 'Of course I'll sign. I'd give anything to play for your team.'

Carey, never a man for overstatement, told the *Sunday*

Chronicle after Edwards' first game: 'He's a good 'un—the best I've seen for his age.' Edwards was literally a prodigy, someone outside the normal course of nature. At sixteen, he possessed the physique and stamina of a man, with huge, tree-trunk legs and a barrel chest. In spite of his size, he had wonderful acceleration, and a turning circle that would have delighted a ballet master. He did not possess the magnetic control that comes naturally to some Continental footballers, but that was his only limitation. His tackling was fair, but ferocious, leaving shaken opponents the impression of having been hit by a runaway steer. His heading had a compelling fascination, with all the timing of John Charles at his best. His passing over long distances matched Haynes for its accuracy: he could skim the ball above the turf to the feet of a player forty yards away. Completely two-footed, he was at home anywhere on the field, and England—who first capped him at eighteen, another record—used him in the forward line when they felt short of firing power, for his shooting was devastating from any distance. Edwards, who trained maniacally, never slackened his pace from the first minute to the last. He could dominate a game through sheer presence: a unique player, quite beyond comparison, whom no adjectives can adequately describe.

While Edwards looked formidable before he even kicked a ball, Dennis Violett often gave the appearance of getting up from a sick-bed—he seemed pale and thin, out of place in a team that bloomed with health. But Viollet, another product of Manchester Schools—ironically, his parents lived a stone's throw from the City ground at Maine Road—became galvanised into activity whenever the ball came near him. His control was superb, and he often slipped through a gap the defence was unaware existed, like a disembodied spirit with supernatural powers. So many of his goals came from colossal cheek, and seemed outrageously unfair . . . to his opponents. Viollet had his first game in the senior side towards the end of the 1952-53 season, when United met Newcastle, after signing professional forms on his seventeenth birthday.

Even frailer was Eddie Colman, a boy so tiny that Whalley, for one, was doubtful whether any amount of skill would compensate for his lack of physique. But Busby and Murphy were keen to give him an extended trial, for they had discovered him all by themselves, when he was playing at wing-half for Salford Boys against Stockport Boys at The Cliff, Broughton. Colman was amazed to be wanted by Manchester United—'I thought I was in the Salford side more or less to make up the numbers,' he said—a modesty that persisted throughout his short career. Although only 5ft 6in, Colman became tough and wiry, revealing great resilience. He had exemplary ball-control, an astonishing flair for the unexpected, and one quality that made him stand out even in a memorable team. Colman's body-swerve, a sort of electronic shimmy from the hips, enabled him to elude tackles and bodychecks in a confined space—invaluable as marking became more and more obsessive. He was nicknamed 'snakehips' by his colleagues, and, as Busby observed, 'he must be the first player who could sell a dummy with his bottom.'

Bill (Liam) Whelan, who first played as an inside-forward for United in March, 1955, at Preston North End, had all Colman's skill with the ball and the height to be a formidable player around the penalty area. Behan,

United's scout in Dublin, sent Busby a note about him while he was with Home Farm, the club that had produced Johnny Carey. Busby had in any case decided to watch a player at Waterford that weekend, so he arrived early to see Whelan take part in a morning match. His first, favourable impression was confirmed by Whalley, who brought Whelan back to Manchester. Because John Doherty was injured, United were short of a player for the second leg of the Youth Cup final against Wolves; a formidable trial which he passed splendidly, although revealing an infuriating, haphazard approach that he never quite overcame.

United beat Wolves 8-4 on aggregate, to take a trophy they were to win five years in succession. A glimpse of the future could be seen in the 1952-53 team: Clayton; Fulton, Kennedy; Colman, Cope, Edwards; McFarlane, Doherty (Whelan), Lewis, Pegg, Scanlon—with six of the players from Manchester itself.

Of course, not even Busby could find a whole team on his own doorstep. Three players were bought from other clubs—Ray Wood, Tommy Taylor and Johnny Berry.

Wood had a frustrating period before he settled at Old Trafford. Born at Hebburn-on-Tyne, he spent two years as an amateur, then touted himself around unsuccessfully at Gateshead, Sunderland and Fulham before Darlington signed him. He was not, at Darlington, an outstanding player: United bought him for £5,000, in December, 1949, because Crompton and Allen were both injured and they were desperate for a goalkeeper. Wood signed at three o'clock in the morning, made his first League appearance in a 1-1 draw against Newcastle twelve hours later, then had to wait until 1953-54 for a regular place. He established himself as a confident, subtle goalkeeper, rarely inspired, always dependable. What he lacked in class he made up in courage—a quality which earned him three caps for England.

Taylor, another former miner, was already an outstanding and successful player when Busby sought his services—both for Barnsley in the Second Division and the British Army, while he was on National Service. Busby and Murphy spent four tense days in negotiations at Barnsley, playing cat and mouse with the Cardiff City manager, Cyril Spiers. Taylor, however fancied United, and Busby managed to beat down the Barnsley chairman, Joe Richards, by one pound—to £29,999, so that his new centre-forward would not be burdened by a £30,000 fee. Taylor arrived at Old Trafford in March, 1953, with his boots tied up neatly by his mother in a brown paper parcel. Within a few weeks he was chosen for the full England side. Taylor was not, intellectually, a clever player, but he had a sixth sense of where a pass would go, and he was so fast, that a hasty clearance to nowhere often seemed to drop perfectly in front of his racing feet. Tall and strong, he had a formidable shot, worked like a trojan, and headed the ball like Dean and Lawton at their brilliant best.

The oldest member of the team, Johnny Berry, whose first job was working the projectors in the Ritz cinema at Aldershot, was one of the first to come to Old Trafford, in August, 1951. Busby became convinced that he must buy Berry after a vital Good Friday fixture against Birmingham City at Old Trafford, which Berry won almost on his own, taking the ball from one penalty area to the other in a meandering dribble past five players before beating the goalkeeper with a ferocious shot. For a time

Busby's overtures to Birmingham brought a curt response, then some eighteen months later, their manager, Bob Brocklebank, telephoned Manchester United. He said, with evident disappointment: 'Our board has agreed to release Berry—at £25,000, not a penny less. He's yours, if you're willing to pay.' Busby needed no second opportunity.

So the team of all the talents was assembled at Old Trafford: Wood, Foulkes, Byrne, Colman, Jones, Blanchflower, Edwards, Berry, Whelan, Taylor, Viollet, Pegg and Scanlon. Even before they won a championship, Bernard Joy, footballer turned journalist, shrewdly observed that in a few years they would be 'strong claimants for the unofficial title of the greatest English club side of all time'.

Where's the pad—I'm his road manager

4

Europe: The Beating of Bilbao

The youngest team in the First Division was now also the best. With only two players, Berry and Byrne, left of the 1951-52 championship side, United regained the title in emphatic fashion four years later.

Taylor was injured at the start of the season, when United took only eight points from their first seven matches, lagging behind the pacemakers, Blackpool, Preston, Charlton and Wolves. But his return, and the introduction of Whelan at Blanchflower's expense, brought a dramatic turn. United beat Preston 3-2, a tremendous boost to morale, then, on October 8, defeated Wolves 4-3 in a breathtaking game at Old Trafford. They were now level on points with Blackpool and West Bromwich, and victory at Cardiff on October 29 took them to the top. Sunderland, running into form, were still spoken of as possible champions, but United beat them 2-1 in a vital fixture on December 3. They began to outstrip their rivals with brilliant football, crushing West Bromwich 4-1 at the Hawthorns on Christmas Eve, then scoring five goals against Charlton Athletic. The first win of the new year, 2-1 at Manchester City, established a four-point lead over their nearest rivals, Blackpool.

Both United—ignominiously beaten 4-0 by Bristol

Rovers—and Blackpool quickly lost interest in the F.A. Cup, and by the end of February the championship clearly lay between them. United's young players went from strength to strength, so much that when Foulkes hurt a leg he could not get back into the team because his deputy, Ian Greaves, was playing so well. Blackpool strained every fibre to reduce United's four-point advantage, and their best chance came at Old Trafford on April 7. Half of Manchester wanted to see the match, and the gates were closed forty minutes before the kick-off with 62,277 crammed into the ground. United were all nerves, dash and splutter, seemingly over-awed by the occasion. Blackpool, cleverly prompted by Matthews. scored first and still led at half-time. But Busby calmed his team in the dressing-room, and they were transformed in the second half. Wood became an interested spectator to a siege of the Blackpool goal, where first Berry (from a penalty) and then Taylor scored. United won by the smallest possible margin, but their superiority was immense—indicated fully by the record eleven-point margin of their championship victory.

In tactics and teamwork United were head and shoulders above any other English side. While, with the possible exception of Taylor, the forward line did not contain any truly great players, together they were formidable. Busby taught them to play with method and precision, to attempt passes that were within their limits, to keep the ball on the ground wherever possible and not to over-reach themselves. He used the team's strength and stamina to achieve mobility, so that the players moving into space without the ball became more important than the man in possession. Their style appeared intricate, with a large and varied number of passes, but it became easy because of the large number of options available to the man with the ball. There were more players to pass to than the defenders could mark, and sooner or later, by constantly moving forward, United created a situation of numerical superiority within shooting range.

For some teams, like the mercurial Tottenham side of the late fifties (*not* the early sixties), the same movement of ball rather than man became stereotyped. Tottenham also concentrated on possession, but were more static, more predictable. Busby used the exceptional talents of Colman and Edwards to vary the approach to goal. Colman could extricate himself from a cul-de-sac which would have baulked most players: Edwards, under pressure from an opponent, could pass with accuracy that was incredible.

Busby already used the 4-2-4 system long before anyone was really aware of it in England, with Colman and Whelan in midfield, Taylor and Viollet forming a double spearhead. It was he, too, who introduced the 'switch' in attack—a forerunner of the 'whirl', whereby ultimately defenders, too, would change roles. Because United could, in a given situation, change expertly from short to long passes, Busby devised a tactic to alter suddenly the point of pressure. For instance, Byrne, Viollet and Pegg might combine on the left flank, with Pegg passing back behind Viollet to Edwards in midfield, who would then find Berry with a long ball on the opposite diagonal. No sooner had the defenders rearranged themselves to combat this new menace, than the process might be repeated, this time with Taylor on a wing and Pegg used as a decoy in the centre.

This blend of Continental finesse and British vigour

was ready for its test against the élite of Europe. The first European Cup had been an outstanding success, gathering momentum in receipts and popularity, with the final televised throughout much of the Continent. Once again the Football League, suspicious of a competition they could not control, advised their champions, Manchester United, not to compete. Politely, but firmly, United rejected their advice. 'We do not fear a congestion of fixtures,' said Busby. 'We have at least eighteen players who can play in the first team without noticeably weakening it.' He told the League that 'the experience gained in competition against the finest clubs in Europe would be invaluable to my young players. After England's two failures in the World Cup, prestige alone demands that the Continental challenge should be met, not avoided.'

In the first round United were drawn against the Royal Sporting Club of Anderlecht, champions of Belgium, managed by the former Blackburn goalkeeper, Bill Gormlie. The first leg took place on September 12, 1956 in Brussels, where the English champions were fortunate to win 2-0. Edwards could not play because of injury, but Blanchflower, in an unfamiliar defensive role, had a superb match, in spite of intense pressure from the Belgian attack. When the score was still 0-0 Jones handled to stop Dewael scoring, and the referee awarded a penalty. Jeff Mermans, Anderlecht's captain and international centre-forward, took a long time over his kick and all but splintered a post. The rebound came straight back to Dewael, but Foulkes, with great presence of mind, had followed him into the penalty area. He took the ball off Dewael's toe, cleared upfield to Colman, and with the Belgians quite unprepared, Viollet glided in to score an astonishing goal. Thereafter Anderlecht, a skilful yet brittle side, played with more desperation than conviction, and Taylor made the game safe with another goal fifteen minutes from time.

This match had attracted little attention outside Manchester, and after United's superficially easy victory, a large crowd was not expected for the return. But 43,635 turned up at Maine Road, used instead of Old Trafford —where the floodlighting system was not yet completed.

They were rewarded for their allegiance by a breathtaking exhibition from United in pouring rain, with pools of water forming natural obstacles on the pitch. After nineteen minutes Anderlecht were holding on to a goalless draw; then they were hit by a whirlwind. United scored four goals in twenty-two minutes, passing with almost divine intuition, shooting with relentless accuracy and power. Week, the courageous Belgian goalkeeper, offered stubborn resistance—but he was beaten ten times by Viollet (4), Taylor (3), Whelan (2) and Berry. After Berry had scored United concentrated on providing chances for Pegg, the only forward without a goal, although he had been on irresistible form at outside-left. Anderlecht grasped the situation and marked him grimly to the end, preventing the total from reaching even more horrifying proportions.

The British press dismissed Anderlecht as mediocre, but to defeat any professional team by ten goals, let alone a champion club, was an extraordinary achievement. Anderlecht, moreover, had beaten Arsenal at Highbury on their previous visit to England. The referee, Mervyn Griffiths of Wales, said he had 'never seen football more deadly in execution'. Busby commented that 'It was the finest exhibition of teamwork I have ever seen from any team—club or international. It was as near-perfect football as anyone could wish to see.' United's win caused consternation on the Continent, and Mermans could not disguise his amazement. 'After they had scored their sixth goal they still ran as hard as they had at the start. We have played against the best teams of Hungary and Russia—and never been beaten like this. Why don't they pick this team for England?' Blanchflower was speechless when the interpreter translated!

United, a little arrogant in victory, nearly paid the penalty in the next round, against Borussia Dortmund of West Germany, in front of an enormous 75,598 crowd at Maine Road. If Borussia were stronger than Anderlecht, they had not shown it in the first tie, in which an amateur club, Spora Luxembourg, took them to a play-off. United seemed ready to start where they had left off, for in thirty-five minutes Viollet scored twice and Burgsmüller turned a shot from Pegg into his own net. But Kwiatkowski, who had borrowed a green jersey from Manchester City's German goalkeeper, Bert Trautmann, made a series of stupendous saves—three at point-blank range that stick in the memory, a combination of instinct and acrobatics—as Taylor and Viollet met passes with all their strength. United attacked and attacked, began to run out of energy, and with Viollet hurt in a clash of heads, found the game slipping away from them. Byrne contemptuously breasted down the ball instead of clearing first time, and Kapitulski gleefully intercepted his back pass. Ten minutes later another defensive error was exploited by Alfred Preissler, whereupon Borussia raged around the United goal and were unlucky not to draw level.

The lead looked slender for the second leg in Dortmund, played at freezing point on a slippery pitch closer to corrugated iron than to grass. United were seriously unprepared, travelling without rubber studs, so their trainer, Tom Curry, had to make a hasty conversion in the dressing-rooms with the only short studs available. Under Dortmund's marvellous floodlights United kept their heads better than their feet, with Wood, wearing tracksuit trousers tucked into his stockings, darting here and there to make desperate saves. Byrne redeemed his mistake at Maine Road with an immaculate display, and Jones held the seams of the defence together with great determination in the intense cold. The most relieved player at the end was Foulkes, who handled in the penalty area to stop Niepielko heading the ball, fortunately on the blind side of the referee. Preissler and Kelbassa each made space and a moment for explosive shots, but Wood was equal to everything and the game ended without a goal. Preissler, Dortmund's captain, was generous in defeat. 'In England Manchester swamped us with incredible football. In Germany they fought like tigers. They will win the European Cup.'

Firstly, however, United wanted to keep the League championship. The following Saturday, November 24, after what had been a mediocre display at Dortmund, they met Tottenham Hotspur at White Hart Lane. The match seemed critical, for the two teams were clear favourites for the title, and victory was effectively worth four points. United fielded the same team as in Germany, for Viollet had not recovered from injury: Edwards again played in the attack, with Wilf McGuinness, another schoolboy international on the fringe of the senior team, filling his role admirably at wing-half. Busby always said that McGuinness played above himself in first-class matches, and he was outstanding at Tottenham, subduing Harmer after Spurs had scored two quick goals and threatened to run away with the match. United eventually drew 2-2, and went on to keep their title six points ahead of Tottenham, in spite of another draw later at Old Trafford.

Although Busby went to see Atletico Bilbao eliminate Honved in the same round, United again underestimated the strength of their next opponents. They had a harrowing flight from Manchester in an old Dakota, with Jones and Whelan very ill during the trip, and Edwards, another poor traveller, looking more and more apprehensive. Foulkes unthinkingly rested his feet on a lever near the bulkhead, which came down when he went to sleep and shut off the heating system. The whole party were freezing by the time they discovered what was wrong, and Harold Hardman, United's seventy-five-year-old chairman, suffered a mild stroke which put him in hospital, compelling him to miss the match. Poor Foulkes was given a special nickname for the rest of the trip: P.B.—Popular Bill.

The plane circled Bilbao in the clouds, and the pilot asked everyone to keep a lookout for the runway—not a move calculated to encourage the green-looking travellers. The British assistant consul, who was decidedly on his toes, heard the plane flying overhead and raced down to the airport—which had been closed because of the poor conditions. He got it re-opened just in time, and the Dakota landed in a blizzard on a deserted field with no terminal buildings; just a dirty old customs shed for two bored, underworked officials.

Walter Crickmer, the club secretary, grimly supervised the Spanish hotel's chef, to whom even English tea seemed an insuperable difficulty. The food still did not suit the players, and Taylor was ill with stomach trouble after eating fried rice, but he kept quiet until after the match.

Bilbao had won only one game since their narrow squeak against Honved, but for all this, they had lost only once on their own ground in three years. The snow came down in little puffs like candy floss, gradually whitening the rows of black umbrellas on the exposed terraces. The ground was waterlogged, and little spurts of spray came up every time a player broke into a trot.

United were a matter of inches from a goal straight from the kick-off, for Viollet splashed through following a superb passing movement and beat Carmelo, only for the ball to stick on what was generally supposed to be the line. The Basques booted clear, and the ball came to Jones, who forgot the conditions and tried to pass on the half-volley. His left foot gave way in the mud, his right missed the ball, and a surprised Arteche, Bilbao's centre-forward, emerged from the jumble of arms and legs with only Wood to beat—which he did.

The two evening newspaper reporters, Tom Jackson and Alf Clarke, snatched up their telephones and began dictating furiously what should have been the opening paragraph of their 'running' stories to Manchester. Unfortunately the local exchange stuck the plugs in the wrong holes, and for a while they were sending their reports to each other across a few yards of the press box, each trying to shout above the other English voice on the line. By the time this hilarious, if critical situation had been resolved, Bilbao had scored again, and, as though

Early days in Europe: Edwards (*above left*) masters Sekularac of Red Star Belgrade, and Gregg (*below*) keeps a dangerous cross away from Schiaffino of AC Milan

BUSBY BOYS

The men of Munich and after: clockwise, from facing page: Pegg, Edwards, Whelan, Jones, Byrne, Wood, Viollet, Ernie Taylor, Setters, Quixall, Dawson and Cope

IN EUROPE

Stiles listens . . . and argues . . . but
Prljaca of Sarajevo is sent off

Despair to exultation: the humours of Denis Law, holding (*overleaf*) the League championship trophy

boosted by some psychological super-charge, dominated the match and headed a third goal before half-time.

However, Busby's eloquence in the dressing-room lifted a depressed United. In eight minutes they scored twice, through Viollet and Taylor, who should not have been playing but was extending the formidable Garay to the limit of his powers. All Taylor's effort seemed wasted when bad marking allowed Bilbao to head two more goals—Manchester were particularly weak in the air throughout this match—to establish an apparently invincible three-goal lead.

However the Spaniards had reckoned without Whelan, who scored a phenomenal goal five minutes before time. He took possession from Edwards inside his own half, did a pirouette past one player in the centre circle, touched the sodden ball past a second, then, still moving on a diagonal from right to left, shrugged his shoulders and rolled over another tackle. He had travelled over forty yards, and had reached the opposite flank when he made a corkscrew turn past a fourth player and accelerated into the middle. Whelan was twenty-five yards out when Garay decided that he merited his attention even more than Taylor; and by then it was too late. Carmelo came out dutifully to narrow the angle, and with Busby quite unable to look, Whelan summoned one last reserve of strength to shoot high into the top left-hand corner. In such conditions, it was an incredible goal.

The Dakota had been left outside during the blizzard, as the one hangar at Bilbao airport was already full. A ground engineer was flown out from England to service the plane, but the pilot took one look at its covering of ice and snow and said flying was out of the question.

Busby, however, was determined to get back to England in time for United to fulfil their away fixture at Sheffield Wednesday on the following Saturday. 'In view of the League's suggestion that United should have nothing to do with the European Cup,' he said, 'I could well imagine the repercussions if we failed to turn up at Hillsborough.'

In desperation, United got the aircraft free of ice with their own fatigue party. All the players grabbed brooms and shovels—except Whelan, who delighted in taking pictures of the team at work, which he sold to a Manchester newspaper after they got back. Lunch was interrupted for a hasty take-off when the local met office reported a break in the bad weather. The flight was, if anything, worse than the outgoing one, with the plane buffeted in a gale, and narrowly avoiding disaster at the refuelling stage in Jersey. There the Dakota dipped frighteningly below a cliff, then, as the pilot opened the throttle, shot over the top to bounce on the runway. Jones sat motionless with sweat pouring down his face, and few of the party looked unperturbed.

'At the very worst,' said Bilbao's manager Ferdinand Daucik, a former Czech international, 'we will have to play-off at Paris. No team can beat us by three clear goals.' As if to reinforce his words, he fielded a defensive side. Uribe, who had scored twice in the first leg, was injured, and wing-half Etura replaced him in the centre.

The atmosphere at Maine Road could be cut with a knife, the crowd was at fever pitch, and United were too anxious. They made frequent errors, squandered two good chances, and the tie seemed to be slipping away. But four minutes before half-time Garay had to kick a shot from Edwards off the line, and Viollet pounced on the rebound to score. The interval ringed with the clamour of excited voices, although most of the forecasts in this improvised senate would have seemed out of place in a temple of logic.

The pulsating pressure continued, with United straining every nerve to tilt the balance. Deutsch, the cool, composed German referee who smothered every potential outburst, courageously disallowed successful shots from Whelan and Viollet, offside decisions that could be measured in millimetres. The crowd bayed for his blood, then concentrated on producing a new volume of support for United. In the seventieth minute, as Busby calmed his mental agony with yet another half-finished cigarette on the touchline, Taylor swerved past a flabbergasted Garay and shot left-footed on the run. Carmelo dived, flailed vainly with his fingers, then gasped with relief as the ball thudded against a post and rebounded to a defender. The crowd groaned in anguish, but Taylor, rising magnificently to the occasion, tried another run past Garay and smashed his shot high and wide of Carmelo for a memorable goal. In unbearable suspense United drove themselves into a frenzy to prevent a play-off. Taylor flew down the wing, with Garay, the last support for Bilbao's tottering edifice, grimly dogging his heels, and again escaped near the corner flag. Berry screamed for the ball, which Taylor, with inhuman composure, rolled gently back to him for a third, sensational score. United, now, could play out time, but the tension tightened another unbearable notch when, in the final minute, Foulkes' back pass fell short and Wood won the race for possession by the smallest fraction. It was enough; Deutsch's last whistle became a mimed signal, and even the radio commentators were drowned by the deluge of sound which rolled around England and into the homes of dejected Basques at Bilbao.

The treble loomed nearer: for United were leading the First Division, and had reached the final of the F.A. Cup. Ironically, while they were humbling the champions of Europe, it was the little clubs who gave them most trouble at home—Workington, beaten only by another of Whelan's individual goals, and Bournemouth, leading at half-time in the sixth round.

In the League a young player called Bobby Charlton* made his first appearance against Charlton Athletic and scored two goals with his left foot, because his right ankle was too swollen to risk a shot. He also scored in the semi-final against Birmingham City, while Taylor was still recovering from a bone cracked in February.

Charlton was among the United players to be briefed by Busby on the exceptional virtues of Real Madrid, their opponents in the semi-final of the European Cup. Busby watched Real play at Nice in the previous round, but he could not convey what he saw to his sceptical players. Charlton, in retrospect, said that Busby was 'so enthusiastic it was almost unbelievable. I discovered that I was building a defensive wall inside myself, for a player wants to see for himself. For instance, the Boss said Gento was the fastest man he'd seen. But what did that mean to Bill Foulkes, who had to mark him? How fast was very fast? As hard as the Boss talked, however many adjectives and comparisons he used, Gento remained nothing more than fast.'

United simply did not believe a team existed that was clearly their superior. For an hour, it seemed they were right, for while Gento often rushed past Foulkes like an

* See Chapter 10.

express train, his centres came to nothing; Byrne, meanwhile, was equal to Kopa's machinations on the other flank. Even Di Stefano seemed destined for a bad day at Chamartin, for every time he got the ball Colman or Blanchflower descended on him, individually or collectively, and took it away. Di Stefano eventually lashed out in exasperation, and was fortunate not to be sent off.

Real might have been a goal down at half-time, for Taylor missed the best chance of the match, but they showed their true potential after the interval. First Gento produced a telling cross which Rial headed neatly into the net from close range. Then Di Stefano, coming more and more into the game, took a pass in midfield and moved towards the wing; Wood made an ill-advised sortie from his goal which Di Stefano saw in a flash and lobbed the ball high against a post and into the net. United responded with renewed pressure, Pegg tormenting Becerril on the left, and Taylor, driving himself on, reduced Real's lead. It looked a moral victory for United until Gento and Rial sent Mateos away, United foolishly held off the tackle, the ball finally ricocheted back to Mateos from Foulkes' body, and Wood's dive was too low and too late.

Real, raising their game in front of a record 130,000 spectators, who produced a waterfall of noise from the towering stands of the Bernabeu Stadium, perhaps deserved their luck. But United remained convinced that the tie could be retrieved again at Old Trafford. Charlton, replacing Viollet, who had a groin injury, recalled that 'we never doubted that we would win, but we were so taken with the spirit of attack that we never considered the possibility of their scoring. When Kopa put the ball into the net you could feel the shock spread across the packed mass of spectators on to the field and through the players.'

Certainly Real did not make Bilbao's mistake of playing defensively in the second leg under Old Trafford's new floodlights. They absorbed United's over-eager attacks and struck with rapier thrusts schemed by Di Stefano. Gento still appeared to have only one trick, to feint to the right and spring to the left, but once in full flight no one could stop him. His control at breakneck pace was unparalleled, and with Kopa having a more convincing match against Byrne, United's flanks were constantly turned. Kopa scored the first goal in the twenty-fourth minute, following two perfect passes, one by Rial, the other by Di Stefano. Soon afterwards Wood could only parry a fierce shot from Gento, and Rial pounced on the rebound.

United's best players were Blanchflower and Taylor, whom Real stopped by blatant obstruction whenever the ball was in the air. There were constant stoppages for fouls and obstruction, the French referee Lequesne awarding fifty-one free-kicks, twenty-nine against Real. When the Spaniards relaxed in the second half, United found their rhythm too late to save the tie. Taylor, again the best forward, scored in the sixty-first minute, and Charlton drew the match near the end. But none of the British players could compare with Di Stefano, whose reading of the play was astonishing, whose artistry created danger out of nothing.

Real's gamesmanship, which earned them possibly six minutes in wasted time, was not restricted to the match alone. They brought in Torres at right-back to replace Becerril, who had been quite unable to cope with Pegg at Chamartin. Torres, though registered in time for the tie, was not a Real Madrid player; he had been loaned by Real Zaragoza for the rest of the season. Busby, annoyed by this breach of ethics, retaliated by watering his pitch, which seemed too dry and hard for United; but Real threatened to postpone the match, so the sprinklers had to be turned off.

Foulkes thought Manchester had run themselves out by over-attacking. 'There is much truth in the theory that you can have too much of the play,' he said. Charlton thought the game was a 'nervy, desperate reaction. Had we been able to condition ourselves to playing normally, as we did for the last forty-five minutes, when I think we were probably as good as we had ever been, I believe we would have done it.' Busby contented himself with the remark that 'A great, experienced team will always triumph over a great, inexperienced team.' Real, who went on to beat Fiorentina 2-0 in the final, averaged twenty-eight, United only twenty-one. Time should have been on their side.

5

Europe: Journey to Disaster

The third leg of the treble, the F.A. Cup final, also proved beyond the reach of Manchester United. After six minutes play at Wembley the Aston Villa winger, Peter McParland, headed hard but not dangerously at Wood from long range. Then, as Wood caught the ball and turned casually away, McParland hurled himself forward for a shoulder charge. The contact, unfortunately, was head to head, and Wood's cheekbone was shattered. In those days before substitutes were allowed, Blanchflower took over in goal—a position he had filled for United on their Danish tour—and played so magnificently that Villa were restricted to two scoring shots.

When United were 2-0 down Busby decided to send Wood, who had been off the field for some time, then playing on the right wing, back into goal. The move was successful, for it released Edwards into the attack, a titanic fury that rocked Villa back on their heels. Five minutes from time Taylor scored from his corner, a curling header that dipped behind Sims' leap, but United could not quite force extra time.

Busby was criticised for delaying Wood's return to his original position, but in fact Wood at no time was fit to keep goal. He could not focus on his right side, and suffered frequent blackouts. United's physiotherapist,

Ted Dalton, gave him a trial outside the stadium after half-time, and Wood missed most of the shots sent towards him. In a tragi-comic incident a cockney kid ran up to Wood offering him a game with his mates around the corner, little knowing that 100,000 spectators were waiting anxiously for him to return to a slightly more important occasion inside.

Although Wood recovered during the close season, he seemed to lose some of his confidence. Certainly, when the 1957-58 campaign began he was not the formidable goalkeeper he had been—he was making uncharacteristic errors that proved costly. Busby reluctantly decided to buy a new goalkeeper, and he spent a record £23,000 on the Irish international Harry Gregg, who came from Doncaster Rovers in December.

At this time United were struggling a little in the League, down in fourth place behind the early leaders, Nottingham Forest. Every club wanted to beat the champions; some of them, Blackpool at Old Trafford, Bolton Wanderers by no less than 6-0, even did. On October 28 Wolverhampton Wanderers won a vital match at Molineux by 3-1, a score that showed their superiority. But United did have four reserves in their team, forced by a sudden epidemic of influenza, the first changes for ten matches.

What illness had forced, Busby now elected to do by choice. When Gregg made his first appearance against Leicester City, Pegg, Berry, Whelan, Blanchflower and of course the luckless Wood were all dropped. Into the team came Scanlon, Morgans, Charlton and Jones—back again at centre-half. United won 4-0, and if they were well behind Wolves and West Bromwich in the League, the old rhythm and determination had returned. Charlton, in particular, responded to the confidence bestowed in him: 'Knowing that I would be picked again even if I played badly, I went forward.'

Whelan could perhaps feel aggrieved at losing his place, for he had been largely the instrument of United's overwhelming 6-0 victory against Shamrock Rovers in Dublin, their opening tie in Europe. Whelan, playing in his home town, toyed with the Irish defence, scoring two goals and making countless chances for others. United led only 1-0 at the interval, and with a strong wind against them, the second half seemed likely to present some difficulty. But even with Goodwin in place of Colman, United's approach work reached astonishing fluidity. Taylor also scored two goals, Pegg and Berry one each in the biggest defeat of Shamrock Rovers for many years.

The return promised a cricket score, but Rovers fought furiously when United, over-confident, relaxed their grip. The final score, with Viollet getting a good goal in each half, was 3-2, which flattered the Irish not at all. Their second goal came from Tommy Hamilton, a fine youth player who had spent some time at Old Trafford. But he had become so homesick that Busby released him from his contract.

Even Colman had been dropped by Busby in an effort to find the best blend for United. But he was restored to favour for the next European tie against Dukla Prague, and gave a brilliant display in Czechoslovakia, dictating the game with intricate footwork. United had taken a three-goal lead in the first leg at Old Trafford, but in the opening half Dukla had given as good as they got, and were beaten more by stamina than by skill. Webster, Taylor and Whelan each scored a goal with fine opportunism, yet the score flattered United and left them uneasy about the return. In the Army stadium, filled to overflowing with Czech soldiers on special duty, Colman slowed and even stopped the play whenever Dukla threatened to get on top. At the other end Taylor was left almost alone against the Czech defence, and played with such vigour, chasing everything however hopeless, that Dukla dared not leave him unattended for an instant. Dvorak scored a fine goal before half-time to raise their hopes, but too many chances were squandered by careless shooting and passing; United, although outplayed, escaped lightly for an aggregate victory.

Again the biggest problem was returning home in time to fulfil a League fixture on the following Saturday. England was covered by a December fog, and B.E.A.'s scheduled flight by Viscount did not not take off on the Thursday. After some desperate telephoning United managed to get enough seats on a Dutch Airlines flight to Amsterdam, the nearest point clear of fog, from where they could travel to England. The press, unfortunately, had to be left behind: their own hard-earned route was by air from Prague to Zurich, Zurich to Birmingham and British Railways to Manchester, a sixteen hour trip on the Friday which would have done Manchester United no good at all. It was this struggle to get home that decided Walter Crickmer to order a charter plane for the next hurdle, against Red Star Belgrade.

First, though, Red Star had to be tackled in Manchester. Here United touched their sweetest form in a clash of titans, for the Yugoslavs had fifteen internationals in their party and played ten, while Busby selected nine internationals and left out five—Wood,

Blanchflower, Whelan, Pegg and Berry. Beara had a magnificent match in the Yugoslav goal, peering through the gloom and making save after save; three of his stops, from Edwards, especially, bordered on fantasy.

United were a goal down at half-time, a marvellous shot by Tasic which came out of nothing. When he was thirty yards out, carefully watched by Foulkes, he made a sudden lunge to the right that caught his opponent off balance. Gregg, feeling Tasic was about to break through, moved off the line to prepare for a possible interception. Tasic must have seen him move, for he did not wait for Foulkes' tackle but let fly, suddenly and explosively. The ball soared above Gregg's head, hit the underside of the crossbar and dropped over the line. It took all United's determination to change the course of the game, with a fine finishing effort by Charlton, and a long-range speculative shot from Colman which caught Beara in two minds.

Busby, however, was pleased with the result. For one thing, Edwards had completely dominated Red Star's most menacing forward, Sekularac, who pinched the ball off him early in the match, dawdled arrogantly in mid-field . . . and was caught by Edwards, whose tackle, while meticulously fair, was quite devastating. Sekularac hit the ground like a sack of potatoes; his contribution to the remainder of the match was negligible.

Equally encouraging was the form of United's wingers, Scanlon and Morgans, in place of the old-established pair, Pegg and Berry. Morgans looked frail, but he could surge electrically past an opponent, and seemed galvanised by the sight of goal. Scanlon was in brilliant form, able to take on any number of players in a confined space and humiliate them all. Against Arsenal at Highbury, the Saturday before the trip to Belgrade, he ran from United's penalty area to the other with the speed of a sprinter, beating defender after defender, and then passed perfectly for Charlton to score. 'It was the most dazzling solo run I have seen,' Charlton said afterwards.

United led 3-0, lost the lead in trying to save energy, then accelerated effortlessly to beat Arsenal 5-4. This double change of rhythm was a true indication of a great side. They had gone ten matches without defeat, were breathing down the Wolves' neck in the League, and set off confidently for Belgrade.

The only problem was an injury to Byrne, who had a pulled thigh muscle, but after an intensive fitness test he proved well enough to play. This was Charlton's first European Cup trip, and the team kidded him so much about the terrible food in Eastern Europe, that he filled his suitcase with packets of biscuits and sweets. When he discovered how good the food was, he sheepishly gave everything to the little girl who cleaned his room.

But Charlton was to defy his greenness in a sensational match which captivated everyone who saw it. Red Star felt their task an easy one and had a fatal lapse of concentration at the start. Taylor chased back for a clearance, two defenders challenged, and the ball rebounded to him. When he flicked forward, Tasic, unaware of the onrushing Viollet, allowed the ball to move gently in Beara's direction. But it never reached him, and Viollet, running in unchallenged, carefully glided his shot into the far corner. Now Red Star had to bring back every man to stem the red tide around their goal, and Sekularac was warned by the Austrian referee, Kainer, after his clumsy tackle had ripped open Morgans' thigh.

United, however, kept their heads in spite of huge provocation. Red Star were left chasing an ever-receding ball, and after fifteen minutes they were lucky to escape a second goal when Viollet headed on a corner from Scanlon and Charlton beat Beara—it was disallowed, narrowly, for offside. United's pressure continued and Charlton took the ball away from Kostic nonchalantly about forty yards out, whirled past two tackles, and shot ferociously from long range. The ball sped past Beara like a bullet, and the crowd buzzed like hornets; it was a long time since they had seen shooting like this. Charlton was now in full cry and two minutes later scored again. Edwards rushed up to take a free-kick within shooting distance, made an embarrassing hash of his kick, but nevertheless found Charlton hemmed in by defenders. He had only a fraction of a second, a fleeting glimpse of the net, but a blur passed Beara and bulged the net, leaving him gaping in total disbelief.

Three-nil down at half-time, 5-1 on aggregate, Red Star pulled themselves together. Kostic scored from well outside the penalty-area, a shot Gregg might reasonably have been expected to stop. Kostic should have scored again two minutes later when Sekularac danced away from Foulkes, but the cannonball swished over the bar by a matter of inches. Red Star were now on top, and United's defence became strained to breaking point. Edwards was everywhere, even bursting the ball with one mighty kick, but too many gaps appeared for him to fill. Tasic and Foulkes had a shattering collision in the penalty area, which resulted in Tasic falling flat on his face with Foulkes right on top of him. Foulkes claimed that Tasic fell over and pulled him down but the referee had heard it all before, and he awarded a penalty.

Tasic took the kick himself and scored, although he had momentary heart failure when the ball brushed Gregg's fingertips.

United's lead survived further erosion until the last three minutes when Gregg became so eager to deprive Tasic of intended possession that he handled outside the penalty area. United called every man back, strung a tight line in front of Kostic, and waited for the ball to bounce back. It didn't. Kostic struck his famous screw shot towards the end player, Viollet, the ball hit him on the side of the head and escaped Gregg's desperate dive. Three-three, but the goal Red Star needed to save the tie never materialised.

It had been no match for the faint-hearted. A dozen players, on both sides, had wounds and black bruises where tempers had raged and niggling incidents boiled over. There were patches of scarlet in the snow, and not only where the red line markings had splayed out under the pressure of racing feet. Spectators, too, were hurt, especially when Kostic missed an open goal and part of the crowd tumbled down the terracing in gleeful anticipation. No one disputed the Slavs' will to win; but it was not as great as United's will to survive.

The team was in high spirits at the British Embassy Club after the match, looking forward to another tremendous clash, with Wolverhampton on the Saturday. Even an exasperating delay, caused when Gregg packed Berry's visa into his suitcase by mistake, did not spoil the happy atmosphere at the start of the return journey. No one knew, as their Elizabethan took off from Belgrade on a bitterly cold morning, that this was the beginning of a nightmare.

6

Munich

Riem Airport, Munich: cold and desolate, a dark silhouette in the snow, with crazy, zigzag marks where tractors clustered round static aircraft. The runway edges had been cleared, leaving strange, straight rivers in a desolate white sea.

The Elizabethan carrying United's jubilant party landed in a blizzard shortly after two o'clock on February 6, 1958. Players, officials and journalists trudged in the direction of the terminal buildings to await the end of refuelling. They had a cup of uninviting coffee, and got warm again just in time to get cold; for by half-past two they were back on the runway. The aircraft gathered speed, with the wheels spouting slush and snow, then screeched and juddered to a halt before the point of no return. Captain James Thain, watching the dials while his co-pilot, Captain Ken Rayment, took the controls, saw that the needles on the boost controls were flickering upwards dangerously. Rayment throttled back and braked, both pilots struggling together to hold the control column forward under the sudden pressure. At 2.34, after taxiing back to the start of the runway, they tried again. This time they half expected to stop, applying the brakes sooner and more easily. The plane had a 'slight technical fault' and its occupants were herded back into the airport lounge.

They were given more indifferent coffee; but few had time to drink it before their flight was called for the third and last time. Most people kept the same seats—the press at the rear of the plane, together with Jones, Tommy Taylor, Edwards and Colman. Only Frank Taylor, who had a queasy stomach after an evening of celebration in Belgrade, did not join them; if it was going to be bumpy, he preferred a backward-facing seat at the front. Across the gangway was Gregg, who had left the card school in the centre of the plane because no one else wanted to play with Yugoslav currency. Behind him, looking tired, were Peter Howard, the *Daily Mail* photographer, and his colleague, Ted Ellyard; on the other side Viollet and Charlton. In the centre, with its irresistible table, sat Byrne, Berry, Wood, Whelan and Blanchflower. Then came Whalley and Busby, a pale figure travelling too soon after illness. Pegg moved past them, leaving his front window seat near Foulkes, Morgans and Scanlon; he decided it would be safer at the rear alongside Jones, whose white face was a measure of his dislike and fear of aircraft.

Gregg had given Blanchflower a German cigarette in the lounge, but it was too late for him to light it, so he put it behind his ear. The stewardess counted heads and found they were one short. 'Not one of mine,' said Tom Curry, United's trainer. Then Alf Clarke, who had been diligently phoning 'copy' to the *Evening Chronicle*, came breathless and red-faced across the tarmac, clambered aboard and strapped himself in. He had sent his last story.

Charlton said to Viollet in the seat next to him: 'I'm not taking my coat off this time.' Byrne, trying to lift the tension, joked: 'It's all or nothing now.' Foulkes had a sudden premonition of disaster, recalling later that he 'was suddenly hit by the strongest possible feeling of foreboding. Somehow I knew that we were not going to make it. I crouched right down in my seat with my head on my chest, and strapped myself in so tight that I could hardly breathe.'

The aircraft roared down the runway, picking up speed, but it was still not airborn. Taylor leaned forward and asked Viollet: 'Can you see if the wheel's gone up yet, Dennis?' But it was too noisy for a reply. Someone began to laugh, without conviction. Berry shut him up with 'It's no laugh; we are all going to be killed.' Foulkes pushed a pack of cards into his pocket as the perimeter fence loomed outside his window, and the throttles gave way to vain, intensive braking. There were fierce bangs and screeches, metal grinding and tearing, the plane sliding and bucking like a panic-stricken steer. Above the noise came Whelan's voice: 'If this is death, I am ready for it.' Then came a fearful crash and the port wing struck the walls of a house and was torn off in flames. The rest of the aircraft continued its wild path of destruction. The right side of the rear fuselage hit a wooden hut with concrete foundations about 100 yards beyond and was torn away with explosive suddenness like the wrath of a giant. The remainder, still attached to the starboard wing, scraped and slithered on, reducing trees to stumps, until one big impact made it spin crazily, like some enormous catherine wheel. Then it stopped, a wreck of jagged metal facing the runway, with carnage and debris marking its path.

Gregg, blood pouring from a small cut on his face, crawled through a small gap and dropped on to the ground. He found he had one shoe missing. Thain and the radio officer, Rogers, ignoring the risk of explosion as flames threatened the escaping fuel, directed extinguishers on to little pockets of fire. Gregg ignored an order to run, scrambled back inside the wreckage and brought out the tiny baby of Mrs Vera Lukic, who had been given a lift to join her husband in England. Foulkes got out too, instinctively ran away from the shattered fuselage, then returned when he found Gregg trying to help Busby. Howard, who had been hurled around the cabin, rescued Mrs Lukic; then Frank Taylor, a grotesque, badly-injured figure in the mud; and finally Morgans, unconscious beneath a pile of wood and metal. Other help came to Blanchflower, who had a dead team mate lying across him, and a cigarette still behind his ear; Wood, trapped by an undercarriage wheel and groaning with pain; Scanlon, submerged beneath the wicker baskets containing the team's playing kit.

One of the motionless figures, Viollet, whose head was gashed open, got up casually and stretched. Charlton, who had been catapulted sixty yards into a field still strapped to his seat, recovered consciousness. He undid his belt, and unthinkingly put his jacket underneath Busby, who was trying to push himself up painfully with one hand.

Seven of the United players were dead. Byrne, the captain; Bent, the reserve full-back; Colman, of the 'snakehips'; Jones, talkative anywhere but in the air; Pegg, amiable and imaginative; Tommy Taylor, his great pal, the tireless Yorkshireman; Whelan, the Irish Catholic. Frank Taylor was the only reporter still living. Clarke, Don Davies, George Follows, Tom Jackson, Archie Ledbrooke, Henry Rose, Frank Swift of England goalkeeping fame, and Eric Thompson had all sat in the part of the plane from which there were no survivors. Three of United's officials were also killed: Crickmer, Curry and Whalley.

Walter Crickmer had been with the club for some thirty-eight years, and secretary for all but six of them. He had a gold medal for services to the game; his contribution to the restoration of Old Trafford was immeasurable. One of his many tributes observed that 'he was a religious man, modest and quietly spoken yet with a cheery word for all. He had a hand in everything . . . but was never there to claim the credit. . . . He was an indefatigable worker and a man of great integrity and personal charm.' The same tribute said that 'Tom Curry was beloved for his fatherly supervision of the players' activities, both on and off the field. Bert Whalley was known and respected especially by the young players for his character and code of living which was a great example to them all.'

The list of casualties was grim and lengthy. Busby was put in an oxygen tent, his chest crushed, his right foot broken; his face had a ghastly pallor and he was not expected to live. There were similar fears for Berry, in a deep coma with a fractured skull and many other minor injuries. Edwards' chance was put at 50-50, because his huge strength and iron will had allowed him to survive injuries that would have killed most men outright. Frank Taylor had multiple injuries and was in danger of losing a leg. Blanchflower's right arm and pelvis were broken; Ray Wood had injuries to head and leg; Scanlon had serious injuries to his left leg and a bad wound in his head. Viollet and Charlton also had head wounds, but in their case delayed shock and concussion did more to keep them confined to the Rechts der Isar hospital.

In the offices at Old Trafford there were only a few administrative staff on duty, patiently telling callers that there were no tickets left for the big game with Wolves on Saturday; they were the first to hear the news. Soon it reached Jimmy Murphy, away in Cardiff for Wales' international against Israel. Although a World Cup-tie, it was an easy match; Murphy, as team manager, had still felt he should be there, even though he had desperately wanted to go to Belgrade. Whalley had sat in his seat, and Whalley was dead. As night fell Murphy went back to Manchester by car, where, appointed acting manager, he would face the agonising task of making the show go on.

The fate of the critically injured, which included the dying Captain Rayment, hung in the balance. Blanchflower took a slight turn for the worse; Busby, Berry and Frank Taylor a turn for the better. Edwards continued to show huge powers of resistance, but his injuries were too severe; although the Germans flew a kidney machine from Stuttgart to Munich, it could only delay his death, not prevent it. Edwards died on February 21, fifteen days after the disaster; many of the hospital staff wept bitterly. For 'Big Dunc', a heroic young figure, captured their imagination in this last crisis as he had captured that of others by his performances on the field. He was good natured, of quiet speech, always unassuming; the model of every boy whose ambition lay in professional football. Charlton thought 'There was no other player in the world like him and there has been no one to equal him since.'

In spite of an inquiry, the cause of the disaster was not explained to everyone's satisfaction. Captain Thain was dismissed by B.E.A., because he failed to check that there was no ice on the wings of the aircraft, and because he allowed Captain Rayment, his more experienced co-pilot, to take the controls. But Thain claimed that the real cause of the crash was slush on the runway and subsequent investigations supported his theory. The Ministry of Aviation later recommended that take-offs should not be attempted where slush existed to a depth of half an inch. B.E.A., sharing the general ignorance of this hazard, made a settlement of £35,000 on Manchester United for the loss of eight players and three officials . . . poor compensation for a disaster that need never have happened. Thain spent more than ten years trying to clear his name, until he was successful in having the inquiry re-opened.

In England the mood was not one of reproach, but of everlasting sorrow. It was shared by the whole of Britain, for television had brought Manchester United into the homes of millions, putting faces to names, sharing in strange intimacy their dynamism and spirit. All over England, all over Europe, February 8 was a sombre Saturday, with teams and spectators standing in a silent tribute to the heroes. Few people, whether or not they cared for football, remained unmoved by the disaster; for many it had a sickening impact of high emotion that stayed in the mind when the frequency of other tragedies had dulled the senses. H. E. Bates, the novelist, found the pulse of the nation in a tribute for the F.A. Year Book:

'At six o'clock, out of pure curiosity, I turned on my television set. As the news came on the screen seemed to go black. The normally urbane voice of the announcer seemed to turn into a sledge-hammer. I sat listening with a frozen brain to that cruel and shocking list of casualties that was now to give to the word Munich an even sadder meaning than it had acquired on a day before the war when a British Prime Minister had come home to London waving a pitiful piece of paper and most of us knew that new calamities of war were inevitable.'

7

Aftermath

With Busby hovering in the valley of shadows between life and death, Murphy put the pieces of Manchester United together as best he could. His immediate priority was a trainer in place of Curry, and Foulkes suggested Jack Crompton, once United's goalkeeper, who was doing well at Luton Town. Murphy doubted whether he would come, but Crompton jumped at the chance, and Luton agreed to release him immediately.

Murphy sent his remaining players away from Manchester, with its constricting atmosphere of grief, to the Norbreck Hydro Hotel in Blackpool, where most of them stayed for six weeks. They were joined there by two new signings, Ernie Taylor of Blackpool and Stan Crowther of Aston Villa. Taylor was regarded as a veteran, but his experience was invaluable, and few could pass a ball more accurately over long distances. Crowther had been Villa's best player in the 1957 Cup Final against United, hard, uncompromising, who hated losing. Neither were in any sense brilliant footballers, but they were the best Murphy could find in a short time. As Bob Lord said, tactlessly but realistically, United could not expect other clubs deliberately to weaken their playing staff, however tragic the circumstances.

Two League matches, against Wolverhampton on February 8 and Aston Villa on February 19, were postponed;

the Fifth Round F.A. Cup-tie with Sheffield Wednesday (United had already beaten Workington and Ipswich) took place in midweek, on February 19. When he sat down to pick the team, poor Murphy burst into tears; so much that he and Busby had worked for had gone. Of the regular team, only Gregg and Foulkes were fit to play. Foulkes recalls that 'Before the match Jimmy Murphy said to me that I would have to be skipper, because there was no one else he could possibly choose. I did not like the idea at all, but that was that. It certainly did not help my nerves.'

Ian Greaves was at left-back, normally third choice to Byrne and Bent; Freddie Goodwin, Ronnie Cope and Crowther formed the half-back line; Colin Webster, Ernie Taylor, Alex Dawson, Mark Pearson and Seamus Brennan the attack. Pearson and Brennan had never previously played for the first team; the others were reserves with limited senior experience. Crowther was signed only just in time to play (he was Cup-tied but received special exemption from the F.A.), and the composition of the team was so uncertain that the programme was printed with eleven eloquent spaces where the names of the players should have been.

United were carried forward from this moment in an unnatural wave of emotion, which rolled on throughout their Cup run and did not lose its momentum until the Final itself. On that February night 65,000 turned out at Old Trafford to will their team to win. As Foulkes said: 'Sheffield had no chance, and I felt sorry for them. I don't think they had any heart for the fight. The crowd was hysterical, and I was not far off being the same way. Shay Brennan got two fine goals for us, and we won easily.'

Brennan scored his first goal at 7.58 p.m., producing

a thunderclap that could be heard all over Manchester. The ball swerved uncannily in the mist, and a woman in front of the main stand crossed herself and said: 'Perhaps one of them gave it a push.' At the end Murphy left the field with tears streaming down his face. Many people in the crowd were crying too, including the girl whose scarf bearing the names of United's players now bore a tiny black square against those who had died.

Bobby Charlton, who had sat around in a daze since the disaster, went to watch Wednesday beaten 3-0 and decided he could have played. He did in the next round, when United had to play away at West Bromwich, a formidable team who had disposed of Arsenal 5-1. But Murphy kept his team back in the dressing-room until the last possible moment, and West Bromwich were already on the field to hear the shattering roar of support for United. The match was drawn 2-2, with Manchester outplayed; so they were in the replay, in which no goals had been scored after eighty-seven minutes, when United were almost out on their feet. But Charlton killed a long clearance from Cope, beat three players in a sinuous dribble, giving Webster an open goal by the far post for another extraordinary victory against all the odds.

Fulham, then a rising team in the Second Division, extended United fully in the semi-final. The first match was drawn 2-2, after Langley had limped from full-back to outside-left; the second, at Highbury, United won 5-3. As the score might suggest, the Fulham goalkeeper, Macedo, played brilliantly in the first game and appallingly in the second. Dawson, aged eighteen, son of a Grimsby trawlerman, scored three goals in the replay, the first such achievement since the 1948 semi-final.

The League championship, however, had to be written off. Even with the help of three Bishop Auckland amateurs, Bob Hardisty, Derek Lewin and Warren Bradley—who was such a success on the wing that England took him on their South American tour a year later—United's resources were overstretched. After Munich only one League match was won, against Sunderland, five were drawn and eight were lost. United finished the season in ninth place, their worst since the war.

Viollet recovered from his injuries in time to play one League match—an overwhelming defeat, 4-0, by the Wolves at Old Trafford—and he was preferred to Pearson in the Cup Final team, probably the wrong decision, given hindsight. United did not play well, gave away a soft goal to Bolton, scored by Lofthouse, and only Charlton, it seemed, might turn the match. Shortly after half-time he struck a ferocious shot which thumped the post high to Hopkinson's left, and rebounded cruelly into the goalkeeper's arms. Hardly had United bemoaned their luck when Gregg could only parry a shot from Stevens—Duncan Edwards' cousin—above his head, and as he turned to gather it Lofthouse charged goalkeeper and ball into the net. Gregg was hurt; but the referee gave a goal. Whatever Lofthouse's intention, he had not executed a shoulder charge within the meaning of the laws, and certainly no referee should have accepted it. So United were beaten, overcome a little by the strain of the occasion—which Busby's appearance at the Final, magnificently courageous as it was, did not help. Foulkes recalled that 'The fact that he appeared to be in a pretty bad state—he looked grey and very, very old—upset me for a start.'

Five days later United lost interest in another competition, the European Cup. Their semi-final opponents, AC Milan, had also finished ninth in the League, but with Schiaffino and Liedholm in their forward line, they were potentially one of the most brilliant teams in Europe. Such potential remained unrealised at Old Trafford, where the occasion may have affected their play. Schiaffino scored a fine goal, but United, without ever dominating the game, won with a shot from Viollet and a penalty kick converted by Taylor. The lead seemed precarious, and so it proved. United, drained emotionally, held on grimly at San Siro until half-time, when Milan had levelled the tie with another goal by Schiaffino; but a penalty, casually taken by Liedholm, opened the floodgates and United were glad to settle for a 4-0 beating. Gregg was fit to play in both matches—United made the tiring journey overland—but not even he could compensate for Liedholm's intuitive work in midfield. Charlton, alas, missed both legs of the tie; when the first took place he was making his second appearance for England, shooting two thunderbolt goals at Wembley from amazing distances; on the day of the return he was playing in Belgrade, a singularly unfortunate choice for England's summer tour. He had a terrible match, and United could have made better use of him at Milan. Still, the defeat looked creditable when AC took Real Madrid to extra time in the final at Brussels, and only lost because *they* did not have Di Stefano.

Busby returned to office the following season, having overcome two crises—the terrible injuries of the disaster itself, and learning of the destruction of his team. No one can really grasp the torment in his mind when he was well enough to know the truth. 'I was lost and sorrowing, and for a short period utterly defeated,' he recalled later. 'A man's help at such a time is not his experience, but his faith and the love and encouragement of his friends. United, particularly, have a great board of directors. I am sure no one has had the backing I have had.'

U.E.F.A. invited United to compete in the 1958-59 European Cup, an *ex-gratia* payment for their services to football, and to the competition itself. United accepted, and had been drawn against the Swiss champions, Young Boys of Berne, before the Football League decided they could not take part, because they were not national champions. The logic was suspect, to say the least, for U.E.F.A.'s rules were their own affair, and in any case had been relaxed to permit other non-champions to compete on several occasions. United appealed successfully to the Football Association, but the League put the pressure on, and a joint F.A.-F.L. Committee—which absurdly included F.A. members who had already voted in United's favour—upheld the League's appeal. Whatever the niceties of the case, it was a shabby episode that reflected seriously on both the ruling bodies.

United, however, gave an apt retort to such petty meanness: they finished second in the Football League in the very season they had been 'not good enough to play in Europe'. Their support was phenomenal—the largest home average in England, total attendances of more than one million.

After some spectacular early successes, 5-2 against Chelsea, 6-1 against Blackburn Rovers, Ivan Sharpe voiced the new optimism in cautious terms. 'The pre-Munich team was smoothly commanding: the present side is more mobile but less consistently methodical. Rebuilding takes time, so it can be said that the re-equipment of Old Trafford's forces has been achieved in a remarkably short period.'

Too much, too soon, perhaps; for Busby was not content with his playing staff. He spent £45,000, then a British record—how trivial the fee appears in these inflationary days—on Albert Quixall, whom Sheffield Wednesday were happy to sell to the highest bidder. Quixall, who had played for England against Wales when nineteen, in October 1953, moved in September, filling Old Trafford to the brim for his first match against Tottenham Hotspur. His natural gifts were unquestionable; whether they could be harnessed efficiently remained to be seen.

Ernie Taylor, immeasurably valuable in the critical days after the disaster, dropped into the reserves and eventually went to Sunderland; the departure of Crowther, hard as nails and of dogged endurance, came a little later, in his case to Chelsea. His place was assumed by McGuinness, already blooded before Munich, but now a cool, indefatigable wing-half in his own right. England chose him against Northern Ireland, and with Charlton and Gregg also selected, United lost heavily to Wolves for the second successive season.

It was only when Scanlon, recovered from injuries, returned at outside-left, and Viollet moved to centre-forward, that United promised, incredibly, to win the championship. Of the three formidable inside-forwards, Quixall was indisputably the most gifted artistically, Charlton the most formidable in terms of scoring potential. But both tended to play as the mood took them, staccato fashion, in brooding spasms; Viollet, technically less of a master, combined mobility and endeavour to keep them going as an integral force. With Bradley exciting and ingenious on the right wing, United had a five-star attack with danger in every point; the defence, with space to work and time to reflect, congealed expertly around the penalty area. Put out of the F.A. Cup by the Third Division club Norwich City—who came within a hairsbreadth of a place in the final—Manchester redeemed themselves by taking twenty-three points from a series of twelve League matches, including a win over Wolves with a last-minute goal by Charlton at Old Trafford, which put them level on points at the top of the table. But with the title within their grasp, United faltered slightly, losing at Burnley and Leicester, drawing at Luton, whose minds were on the Cup Final. Wolves did not relax and kept the championship for another stab at European football.

In the following season United showed indifferent form, for indifferent results. Greaves and Goodwin were injured; then, in January 1960, McGuinness's career ended when he broke a leg. He became assistant trainer, a sad loss to England as well as his club. In the first week of December Busby had sent for Charlton, Bradley, McGuinness and Gregg and told them they had been dropped: three of the young men pitchforked into the team after Munich, Pearson, Brennan and 'Dreadnought' Dawson, now claimed places in their own right. Into goal came David Gaskell, another product of the youth scheme, who had been baptised in a Charity Shield game against Aston Villa long before and generously had given the injured Wood his medal.

Wood, though, had gone to Huddersfield Town. There were other departures, Morgans to his birthplace, Swansea, Scanlon to Newcastle, Lincoln and Mansfield. Blanchflower and Berry's careers ended at Munich. In place of McGuinness, Busby signed Maurice Setters, the forbidding *enfant terrible* of West Bromwich Albion, for £30,000. Setters, strong in mind and body, added stability to the defence; Charlton, restored to the team, effervescence to the attack. England had used him, largely in desperation, as an outside-left at the end of their disastrous South American tour. Busby followed their lead, although as Charlton put it, 'there was not an unhappier outside-left in the whole of the League'. But Charlton curbed his excursions into the centre, and eventually won back his England place . . . at outside-left.

United did a little better in the F.A. Cup, narrowly losing to Sheffield Wednesday in the Fifth Round, but were flattered by seventh place in the League. Only Viollet, who broke Rowley's record of thirty goals in a season at Craven Cottage, could look back on the season with much satisfaction. Real Madrid met Manchester home and away in friendlies, winning overwhelmingly at Old Trafford, fortuitously at Chamartin. The score in Manchester was 6-1, where Real fielded a Hungarian (Puskas), two Argentinians (Di Stefano and Dominguez), a Uruguayan (Santamaria), two Brazilians (Canario and Didi) and five Spaniards, an irresistible blend of South American and European styles. In Madrid United rose above their disappointing form, led 3-2 at half-time and lost only by 6-5: a good omen for a more serious affair in the future.

United stayed where they were in 1960-61, seventh in the League, beaten in the Cup by Sheffield Wednesday—although the defeat was earlier and more catastrophic, 7-2 in the Fourth Round. The League position deteriorated in 1961-62, United losing eighteen matches, eight of them at home.

CUP goals Stiles huffs and puffs but Benfica's Eusebio flashes the ball past Gregg

Herd (*above*) tries to break the net in scoring his third goal against Vorwärts

Stiles has sneaked the ball in from the by-line and the Partizan goalkeeper, Soskic, is not amused

Gregg is slow to act and José Augusto (*right*) puts Benfica ahead at Old Trafford

Through the eye of a needle: Gornik defenders grope in vain for Kidd's tantalizing shot

A fusillade of snowflakes as Stepney comba
Lubanski and the weather in a Polish blizzar

A fleeting chance and Best finds a gap, giving the Real Madrid goalkeeper, Betancort, no hope at Old Trafford

The Final: Charlton, Coluna and the Italian Referee, Lo Bello, exchange formalities before the kick-off

Manoeuvres: Charlton and Crerand (*above*) prepare to take a free-kick, Jose Augusto and Eusebio prepare to stop it . . . and no one has time for the injured Best. Crisis for United (*below*) as Murphy and Busby ease the tension before extra time

Frustration for Sadler (*far left*) as Henrique smothers the ball at his feet

Crisis for Benfica as Best breaks clear to score United's second goal. Henrique, failing to intercept, flings himself back in an unavailing dive

Henrique parries Kidd's first header, but the second leaves him helpless and scores off the crossbar to put United 3-1 ahead

The triumph: Stiles grins famously, Charlton is too overwhelmed to smile. (*Right*) A heady moment for Sadler with the European cup

Busby, who had tinkered about with transfers, now decided to commit himself completely to the market. While the youth policy had been re-established—with Quixall dropped, United's team in 1962 had an average age of twenty-one and only Setters had cost a transfer fee —the quality of the players, with certain exceptions, was not as high. Busby had depended more on the grooming of his trainer, Whalley, than perhaps he knew. Matt had an eye for raw talent, but he was less capable, or had lost some of his energy, when it came to bridging the yawning gap between youth and first team football. For a time, too, the Manchester magnet had faded; it no longer could attract every boy in Britain. There were other, more exceptional teams, like Tottenham Hotspur, winning Cup and League in the same season for the first time this century.

8

Europe: Failure Abroad

Erratic and exasperating in the League, Manchester United found their true form in the F.A. Cup, reaching the final for the third time in seven seasons. Again the team bore little resemblance to its predecessor: it was the most expensive ever to play at Wembley, six players costing more than a total of £300,000. Quixall and Setters had commanded £75,000; further big fees were paid for Noel Cantwell, Arsenal's David Herd, Denis Law and Pat Crerand.

Cantwell, born in Cork, was signed by West Ham from Cork Athletic in 1952 and made 245 League appearances for them in eight seasons. When he was transferred for nearly £30,000, a record fee for a full-back, there were some who suspected he was over the top; but this was merely his style of play, cautious, responsive, never naked aggression. Busby was so impressed by his adaptability that he tried him on the left-wing for a few matches in 1960-61, but the move did not have its desired effect. Cantwell went back to left-back, a position he kept either in the first team or the reserves until in 1967-68 Coventry City appointed him manager in succession to Jimmy Hill.

Herd, Law and Crerand* all cost even more—£32,000,

* See Chapter 9.

£115,000 and £56,000 respectively. Crerand's fee was a record for a half-back, paid to Celtic in March, 1963, twenty-one games before the Cup Final: Law's was an all-time record for a British footballer. It seemed a huge sum at the time, with Manchester City making £100,000 out of Torino and Torino selling him to the club 'across the park' at a small profit in July 1962. But while United were winning the Cup ten months later, City were dropping into the Second Division; the respective profit and loss far exceeded even this transfer fee, as Busby pointed out.

Law was signed to add striking power to United's attack, the serious deficiency in the superb teamwork that had troubled Tottenham Hotspur in the semi-final of the season before. Busby said later that 'Although we were erratic in the League, I felt sure that this match was the turning point, the old flair and style were returning. Even in losing, I was confident of the future.'

United scored twelve goals and conceded two on the way to the 1963 Cup Final. They put five past their former goalkeeper, Wood, against Huddersfield; beat Chelsea and Aston Villa each by the odd goal; then won 3-1 at Coventry, majestically brushing aside the goal scored by Bly, one of Norwich City's famous team in 1959. Quixall, who had scored in every round, missed the semi-final through injury, and it took a remarkable opportunist goal from Law to dispose of Southampton at the first attempt.

The Big Freeze, which reduced the fixture list to a fiasco, delayed the final until May 25, when Quixall was fit to play. By this time United had avoided the indignity of relegation, which at any early stage seemed a real possibility. They ultimately finished nineteenth, narrowly ahead of Birmingham City, who, however, were well clear of Manchester City and Leyton Orient.

Busby chose three Republic of Ireland internationals —Cantwell and Tony Dunne at full back, John Giles at outside-right. Dunne replaced Brennan, who was desperately unlucky not to play in the final, one of only seven games he missed all season after moving from outside-left to right-back. His luck would change, however, five years later, for the European Cup Final, also at Wembley.

Giles, while not a particularly outstanding winger, was the best available. He turned professional with United in 1958, after Whalley had reported favourably on his performances for Home Farm, the Dublin conveyor-belt of talent. Giles first appeared in September 1959 at inside-right, where his sudden acceleration and ability to wriggle through gaps seemed more effective. But Busby tried him on the wing, Eire gave him a full cap before his nineteenth birthday in 1960, and there he stayed.

Busby persevered with Gaskell in goal, after toying with the idea of recalling the more experienced Gregg, who lost his place in the semi-final. So Gregg lost his chance to make up for the defeat of 1958, an opportunity which fell to Foulkes, playing in his third final. Foulkes had been something of a passenger early in the 1958-59 season, but the rest of the team had been playing so well that Busby took no action until the defence threw away a point in a 4-4 draw with Newcastle. He suggested that Foulkes should have a rest then try playing at centre-half in the reserves. Foulkes did so reluctantly, liked his new position, survived a sending-off against Chesterfield (from which he was completely exonerated) and won a first-team place at centre-half after United had lost at Burnley.

Foulkes, however, 'had made up my mind on one point. I was going to resign the captaincy of the club. It had been thrust on me in the first place, and the burden had contributed to my loss of form. The Boss asked me to leave it to the end of the season, but I insisted. Mr Busby is a man who does not like trouble, but likes to see everything running smoothly and efficiently. He was rather distressed by my attitude. But I wanted to get the whole thing over and done with, and when it was, I felt very much better for it. Since then Dennis Viollet, Maurice Setters and Noel Cantwell have been captain, and I don't think it has helped the play of any of them.'

Gaskell; Dunne, Cantwell; Crerand, Foulkes, Setters; Giles, Quixall, Herd, Law and . . . Charlton. Although Charlton still had misgivings about playing at outside-left, by now he was an automatic choice for England in this position. He had been one of the few English successes in the 1962 World Cup in Chile, where he had been voted the best left-winger of the tournament. Certainly his absence, because of a hernia operation, contributed to United's lamentable start to the 1962-63 season.

After their showing in the League, United's performance in the Cup Final against Leicester City was a revelation. Gaskell proved horribly nervous, and kept dropping the ball at the start, but Cantwell and Foulkes kept their heads and it was Leicester's nerves that eventually got the better of them. Soon Charlton had Banks, already England's goalkeeper, diving full length, and within a few minutes United were ahead. Crerand beat three players, turned a pass across the penalty area, and Law, shielding the ball with his body, turning stunningly in a tight circle for a sudden and brilliant shot past Banks. He almost got another before half-time, McLintock kicking off the line; this only delayed the inevitable, a cross by Giles from the right, a shot from Charlton on the left. Banks could not hold the ball, which rebounded to Herd, who made no mistake. Leicester rallied with a fine goal from Keyworth, diving recklessly to head the ball past Gaskell as Dunne swung his boot to clear; but United showed just how much they had in hand when Law swept upfield, fed Herd, ran forty yards for the return and headed hard against the post. If that was ill luck, it was balanced when Banks, trying to watch the airborne Law and Giles' cross simultaneously, neither grasped Law's harmless position nor the ball and Herd accepted the open goal. United had risen to the occasion; now they had to rise to the challenge of Europe.

United had an easy baptism against Willem II, a Dutch club who had been in the Second Division when they won the Cup. The first, rather mediocre leg was drawn 1-1 at Rotterdam, Herd scoring a good goal; but United put on the pressure for the return and the Dutch defence collapsed. Law, elusive and arrogant, scored three memorable goals to settle the tie. Willem were never in tune with the pace of the game and even their goal in a 6-1 defeat came from an unfortunate deflection by Cantwell. United could be well satisfied with their performance, in particular that of two young players, Phil Chisnall, who went to school less than 200 yards from Old Trafford, and David Sadler.

Tottenham's victory in the European Cup-Winners' Cup final against Atletico Madrid permitted England to enter two teams, who, by an unkind twist of fate, were drawn together in the second round. Tottenham were without Danny Blanchflower, soon to retire, and the unpredictable and often fallible Marchi assumed both his position and the captaincy. The pulsating tie took place in December, attracting 57,447 to the first leg at White Hart Lane. United played unashamedly to restrict Spurs lead, which seemed likely to be a single goal from the indomitable Mackay until Dyson seized on a defensive error near the end. Few expected United to earn more than a play-off in the return, but the course of the game was decided by a serious injury to Mackay, who broke a leg in a tackle. Thereafter United had Tottenham on the run, Herd scored two fine goals and Charlton two more with marvellous shooting, and a goal by Greaves proved largely irrelevant. Tottenham tried hard, but the handicap of playing with ten men—substitutes were still not permitted—was too great: for the first time the holders were knocked out before the final.

But Manchester lasted only one more round, against Sporting Club of Lisbon. Their elimination was astonishing, for in the first leg at Old Trafford, seen by more than 60,000, United won 4-1, a margin that scarcely indicated their superiority. Law scored three goals, two of them from the penalty spot, and Charlton the fourth in a match marred by error and counter-error.

However the strain of playing for three trophies, League, Cup and Cup-Winners' Cup, was becoming too great for their inexperienced team. Liverpool had set a hot pace in the League, which in running terms United matched at the expense of depriving themselves of a finishing burst. If an exceptional performance by an opponent required them to raise their game, they had nothing left to give.

The cracks began to appear when United, after sweeping through three rounds of the F.A. Cup, needed two replays to dispose of Sunderland, an energetic but far from formidable side. Then, in the semi-final, they fell foul of West Ham at their magnificent best—which even George Best, still finding his feet in first-class football, could not disturb. In driving rain and clogging mud Moore had a brilliant match, making the third, decisive score for Hurst with an incredible advance from the rear, strength and skill compounded, eluding two forwards, hugging the touchline and passing with remarkable accuracy.

United, a tired and dispirited team, travelled to Lisbon with little stomach for a fight. Gaskell's uncertainty in goal spread an infectious disease of indecision throughout the defence; the forwards seemed all misdirected energy, with Herd unhappy and ineffective at outside-right, Law too versatile for an immobile goal-hanging role at centre-forward.

Sporting Club. while not on Benfica's level, had several fine players—in particular Morais, a deep-lying left-winger with superb ball control, but a reputation for ruthlessness; Mendes, captain and wing-half, exceptional in passing and interceptions; and Hilario, a fast two-footed full-back, as good as any defender in Europe. Yet the team as a whole was unbelievably erratic. They had lost 2-0 to Atalanta Bergamo of Italy (who also hit the post three times), wiped out the deficit and won the play-off; annihilated a little Cyprus team, Apoel Nicosia, 16-0 in a snow-storm (Mascarenhas scored six goals) yet won only 2-1 in the second leg.

Any ideas that United might have had about coasting to overall victory were dispelled in Sporting's furious opening attacks. After two minutes Oswaldo Silva scored from a penalty, then again after twelve. The crowd, more than 50,000, fairly buzzed with excitement, but with more luck than judgement United managed to hang on until half-time. Yet their attack was completely subdued, and with the ball bobbing continuously around their penalty area, another goal seemed inevitable. It came within two minutes of the restart, when Geo floated a free-kick over the heads of a defensive wall past the harassed and motionless Gaskell. United's resistance collapsed, Morais put Sporting ahead on aggregate seven minutes later, to be followed by Silva's third goal on the hour. At 5-0 Sporting relaxed and became more cautious, but at no time did United promise a revival. They were beaten out of sight and out of mind.

The press were hard on Busby, for failing to close up the game, and United, for their lack of resilience and will-power. But as Foulkes said, 'United were dog-tired with all the extra games—most of them played in the mud—and the travelling. Our spirit had reached a very low ebb. Even if we had gone out and tried to play a defensive game, to protect our lead, Sporting would still have beaten us. They had one of those nights when everything goes right, and would have beaten any team in the world.'

Sporting went on to win the final, beating MTK Budapest after a replay. United had to be content with second place in the Football League, four points behind Liverpool, which at least gave them entry to Europe's third international club competition, the Inter-Cities' Fairs' Cup.

Here, in 1964-65, Manchester swept through to the semi-final, varying mediocrity with devastating brilliance. Their first opponents were Djurgarden, a fine Swedish team who had lost their championship to Malmö F.F. only on goal average and were to win the title in 1965. Djurgarden played with great determination at the start, surprised United's defence with the excellence and speed of their passing, and made four good chances. Fortunately for United, Pat Dunne, their Republic of Ireland goalkeeper signed from Shamrock Rovers, showed some inspired touches to stop shots at point-blank range. Djurgarden still looked faster than United, and scored through Johannson, their clever left-winger; but their impetus slowly faded, their stamina—they were all part-time professionals—gave out late in the second half, when John Connelly, signed from Burnley, came more into the game. But United left their equaliser from Herd until the last possible moment, and played embarrassingly badly. The constrained atmosphere may have affected their concentration, for there were only 2,000 people in the ground, who produced scarcely a dull murmur. It was the mid-season break in Sweden, when many people went to their summer houses; and in any case Cup football has no appeal, for even the Swedish F.A. Cup died a natural death in 1953.

Just how poorly United had played was seen in the return leg, which they won 6-1, hitting five in the second half, with Law, Charlton and Best quite irresistible. Law scored three goals, one of them from the penalty spot, and Charlton two in a superb performance. Djurgarden had looked fast in the first match, but then they were bewildered and overwhelmed by lightning flicks and touches, science combined with imagination; goals contrived and scored quicker than the eye could see or the brain could anticipate.

Borussia Dortmund, who had won the German championship in 1963, and were to win the European Cup-Winners' Cup in 1966, should have been more formidable opposition. Sigi Held was still to be discovered, but they had the canny Konietzka in midfield; Emmerich, with a left foot like the thunder of Thor; and the impassable Paul at centre-half. Borussia, too, had benefited from the introduction of a proper national league in West Germany, which had speeded up play and brought the best teams into direct competition.

United had been hard put to earn a goalless draw at Dortmund eight years and two months before, in the European Cup itself. But any thoughts of a dour battle of attrition vanished almost immediately. If Borussia had risen in status, giving their players individual dressing-gowns and slippers in their dressing-room, their elegance this day looked an empty shell. United, weathering an anxious ten minutes, overwhelmed them in an hour. Herd opened the scoring, followed by Charlton, Best and Law. Charlton scored three tremendous goals, punishing the slightest error in the German defence. Borussia were quite thankful to settle for a 6-1 defeat; even their solitary goal, by Kurrat, was a doubtful penalty. United methodically took them apart, and started where they had left off in the second leg at Old Trafford. Borussia brought in Tilkowski, later to keep goal against England in the World Cup final at Wembley. But even his reactions were not equal to United, who won 4-0, Charlton scoring twice more, Law and Connelly the others. Beating a team like Borussia by 10-1 was an incredible performance; and United's performance, especially in Dortmund, had to be seen to be believed.

The third round produced an all-English tie against

Everton, a colourful, exciting team but uncertain away from home. But in a fine match at Old Trafford, seen by nearly 50,000, both sides tried too hard and their skills were largely cancelled out. Everton, who had contemptuously eliminated Kilmarnock in the previous round, played tightly in defence and broke dangerously whenever the chance presented itself. However, United seemed on top until Foulkes prepared to trap an easy loose ball on the halfway line, saw Law racing into an open space and passed mentally instead of physically. The ball hit a bump in the ground, reared over his right foot, and Pickering, off the mark like a sprinter, tore through the gaping hole in United's defence. All the Everton supporters yelled at him to shoot, for Foulkes was thundering behind in pursuit, and Pat Dunne had advanced perfectly to narrow the angle. But Pickering left his shot to the last possible moment and slipped the ball past Dunne for all the world as though it were a practice match.

With Foulkes wishing the ground would swallow him up, Gabriel levelled the score in errors. For eighty minutes he had played superbly, but now, with no one near him, he decided to pass a long way back to West. The ball slowed on the turf and Connelly was on it like a flash to draw the match.

Even a draw, however, augured ill for Manchester, who had scarcely a point to show for a dozen visits to Goodison Park. But Law had a superb match and Everton spent so much time and effort watching him that Connelly and Herd were left fatally unattended.

Because of the clumsy arrangements of the competition, six clubs remained after the third round ties had been completed. They were reduced to four by giving byes to two clubs, Atletico Madrid and Juventus, who were to form one semi-final; and making the remainder meet in a special fourth round, Ferencvaros and Atletico Bilbao, Manchester United and Racing Strasbourg.

The French club should have been worthy opposition, for they held third place in the League, and had eliminated AC Milan, Basle and Barcelona (after three draws, two in Barcelona, with Racing winning the toss after extra time). But United destroyed Strasbourg in France, winning 5-0 after an anxious quarter of an hour. Law scored two goals, others came from Connelly, Herd and Charlton, whom Busby decided to play in spite of a stress fracture that had been thought sufficient to keep him out of England's summer tour. Law, European Footballer of the Year, played with demonic energy and showed deadly finishing. The crowd of 29,000, enormous by French standards, gave United a standing ovation at the end.

Yet Manchester, beating Leeds United for the League championship on goal average, lost their magic as quickly as it had come. The return with Strasbourg was poor reward for the 34,188 spectators—a remarkable crowd with the tie a foregone conclusion. Racing evidently thought so too, for they made no attempt to attack, massed in defence and defied United to winkle them out. United, plagued by their constant inability to turn superiority into goals, could not find their touch, and the game became a dreadful, goalless anti-climax.

Ferencvaros came to Old Trafford with an unjustified reputation, for they had needed three games to dispose of Wiener Sportklub and the struggling Atletico Bilbao. They were top of the Hungarian League, but Florian Albert, the master footballer, was in poor form, and his indifferent displays affected the whole side. Ferencvaros were particularly weak on the wings, for Dr Maté Fenyvesi was a veteran and Ratkai and Karaba had been tried on the right without success. Much depended on Rakosi, a brilliant footballer with astonishing finishing powers however tight the space in the penalty area.

The F.A. permitted United to play the semi-final out of season, and the first leg did not take place until the last day in May, when most of their players were wistfully thinking of holidays. With a weak referee, the game rolled along barely on the right side of a riot; as Foulkes said candidly, United 'were just as much to blame as the Hungarians, but the ref made such crazy decisions that the game got out of hand.'

Law scored first from a penalty, and although Novak came out of defence to put Ferencvaros back in the game, Herd gave United a 3-1 lead in the second half. But just when Manchester seemed to have a satisfactory margin to take to Budapest, Rakosi lobbed the ball into the goal-mouth, and Pat Dunne completely misjudged its flight, allowing it to bounce gently into the net. One goal did not seem likely to be enough.

The trip to Budapest went badly from the start. United were stranded at London Airport by a strike, and spent five hours in the transit lounge. Then they suffered another, inexplicable delay at Brussels, where they were to change planes for Budapest. But they had almost two days to recover and remained confident of victory.

Such confidence might have proved justified but for an extraordinary decision by the referee one minute before half-time. Albert had been getting the worst of a duel with Foulkes—against whom the referee awarded several free-kicks, though it was five of one and half-a-dozen of the other. For once he got the ball to Varga, who ran hard against United's massed defence, despaired of finding an unmarked player, and let fly. As Pat Dunne jumped to save the ball hit Nobby Stiles* unmistakably on the shoulder—too hard and quickly, certainly, for him to handle it, even if he had tried to. But the referee awarded a penalty, which Novak converted. United put on the pressure in the second half, but could not score.

Crerand and Orosz, Ferencvaros' left-half, began pushing and shoving each other in midfield, and when the referee did nothing to calm them, both lost their temper. After one incident, which bore little relation to the position of the ball, they had a kicking contest in midfield; even the referee could not ignore that, so off they both went on the long trudge to the Nepstadion tunnel.

According to the prevailing rules, there was nothing to prevent a player sent off from appearing in the next tie, so both Crerand and Orosz took part in the play-off. The clubs tossed for right of venue, and when Busby returned from the dressing-room with a long face his players knew they would have to come back to Budapest.

Again the trip was a nightmare. United flew to Vienna with comparatively little delay, but the remainder of the journey was to be made by road. The Hungarian customs searched their coach with maddening and fruitless efficiency, so two hours and a half elapsed before they were allowed over the border.

There had been torrential rain in Hungary for days, and the hotel where United intended to stay at Budapest, situated on an island on the Danube, had been threatened by floods and evacuated. The main road, too, was flooded, so United's Austrian driver phlegmatically

* See Chapter 9.

set off across country, on dirt track roads through rustic villages, dodging chickens, children and country yokels. Foulkes recalled that 'In one town, Gere, we followed the arrow pointing to Budapest down a narrow back street and finished up in a field. Our driver followed the ruts made by a tractor, and they eventually ended up on the road again. I turned round and looked at the Boss, whose expression spoke volumes. It seemed we just could not win this one.'

Nor could they. Within five minutes Connelly produced a perfect pass for Law, who had only Geczi to beat; but he hesitated, and Matrai, recovering superbly, whipped the ball away. United still made all the running, but lacked sharpness near goal. Again, one minute before half-time, Ferencvaros scored out of no apparent danger. Karaba, who had scarcely been allowed a kick by Tony Dunne, gave up trying to pass him and shot from at least thirty yards. The ball swirled and dipped into the net at the closest possible point to the junction of post and bar, leaving even Pat Dunne, who had a splendid match, quite helpless. Karaba was overwhelmed by his teammates, but as pictures showed later, the shot had gone yards away from its intended direction.

United remained impotent in attack, and soon Ferencvaros scored again. Karaba shot from close range, Brennan booted clear, but only back to Karaba. His second shot rebounded from Stiles' body straight to Fenyvesi's left foot. He was standing unmarked and simply could not miss. Ferencvaros wrongly assumed the game was over, for when Connelly scored in the last ten minutes, United had enough chances to snatch victory out of the fire. But Charlton, taking a lucky rebound, hit a ferocious shot a foot too high to trouble the petrified Geczi. Then Best, who had beaten six players (one of them twice) in a sinuous, electric dribble, tried one feint too many and fell over the goalkeeper's body; the ball rolled on towards the net, but Matrai cleared desperately. When Herd missed another easy chance in the final minute United's last hope had gone.

Ferencvaros went on to win the Fairs' Cup, beating Juventus on their own ground in Turin. Fenyvesi again scored the decisive goal, on the half hour, but few people really cared. At their best United could have taken the trophy, and might have done with fewer mistakes and exacting fixtures. But they were League champions, and ready to take on Europe for the greatest prize of all.

Is he good?—he sold me £20's worth of gear at half-time

9

The New United

The failure, by Manchester United's own highest standards, in Europe nevertheless afforded Busby a breathing space. It gave young players an insight into the tension and peculiar problems of competing with the Continent, and it gave their manager time to experiment with particular combinations and to weigh up an individual's potential.

In a sense the inability to produce another set of brilliant youngsters out of a hat was inevitable. Busby himself was under no delusions that it was easy. 'What we always need in particular,' he said, 'is some good luck. The world's best pickers of promising lads still make a mistake in their estimate of how far even the most promising will go. Everyone hears about our successes: little has been said, because we don't shout about it from the roof-tops, of our failures. Take it from me we have had our big failures. Nobody can forecast, with certainty, whether any developing lad has it in him to go the last yard.

'Don't let anyone run away with the idea that our method of team building is cheap or easy. In one season, for example, our scouts watched well over five thousand youngsters. Of these only about three hundred were eventually thought to be promising enough to be invited for trials. And of these less than a dozen seemed good enough to justify the grooming.'

The difficulties were increased because of Busby's particular requirements, modified by the experience gained from the opening campaigns in the European Cup. For him, speed and strength were of secondary importance. He wanted players 'with an ability to read the game, and play it mentally without the ball'. He wanted footballers with exceptional ball-control, the basic skills to beat the hazards and vagaries of British conditions. Above all he was looking for 'adaptability, for example when all forwards can play in all forward positions'; soon it went further than that—soon he wanted players who, barring goal, could play anywhere. Versatility, a constant switching of roles, enabled a team to change the point and personnel of attack without losing their fluidity.

Much is made of United's inherent skills, but many of these have been improved, even discovered, by intensive coaching. McGuinness represented Busby's view when he said that he 'quickly learned that coaching was *not* optional. Players *must* be coached, just as actors must learn their lines. Coaching is not a luxury, nor an idea to be played with. It is an absolute necessity.

'Every player has something that can be improved in his game. In every player there are faults to be removed. The relevance of coaching to the professional is much more, in fact, than to youngsters. It teaches a player the tactics of the game . . . it opens up a player's mind, as well as his skills.'

Perhaps the most coached, and the most versatile of the new United was Shay Brennan, the only stop-gap after Munich ultimately to hold his place. He has played for

United at outside-left, inside-forward, centre-forward, wing-half, left-back and right-back—and been given different preparations for them all. Although Brennan's parents are Irish, he was born in Manchester and went to St John's school at Wythenshaw, where he played in the forward line. His first job was as a joiner, which did not make heavy demands on his free time; he continued playing for the Old Boys' club, in the South Manchester and Wythenshaw League, where he was seen by both United and City. Manchester City got to him first, but Brennan was a United supporter. So 'I hung fire and hoped that United would approach me very quickly.' They arrived two days later and offered him a job on the ground staff, which he accepted immediately.

Brennan of course came into the team after Munich as a left-winger, scoring direct from a corner with a strange, swirling shot against Sheffield Wednesday. But he lost his place before the semi-final, and although he played in the replay at Highbury, there was little question of him appearing in the final. In February, 1959, he asked Busby if he could try a move to wing-half; this was relatively successful in as much as he returned to the League side for the last match of the season, against Leicester City.

The following season he was back in the reserves. He only played when Goodwin or McGuinness were hurt, or lost form. Even a long run in the first team from November, 1959, was ended by the arrival of the England Under-23 captain, Setters. Brennan eventually found his niche at full-back, where he competed for a place with Cantwell and Tony Dunne. Although he did not play in the 1963 Cup Final, Brennan eventually took over at right-back—Busby switching Dunne back to the left with great success. England actually nominated Brennan for their World Cup forty in 1962, but the Republic of Ireland capped him on the basis of his father's nationality. Under F.I.F.A. rules Brennan cannot play for a second country, even though he was born in England and only goes to Ireland on holiday.

Dunne, not related to United's goalkeeper, Pat Dunne —although both were born at Dublin—came into the senior team during the 1961-62 season, his style is a complete and effective contrast. Where Brennan is cool, Dunne is dashing and impetuous, but with such staggering powers of recovery that he can get away with the most audacious advances into attack. There may have been more decisive full-backs in England, but no one as fast. Even when beaten, Dunne shows that he can recover in a flash for a second tackle, often taking the ball casually away from a disbelieving winger.

Busby built a new partnership in defence by moving Foulkes to centre-half and introducing a little man in close support called Norbert Stiles. Comic in appearance, controversial in character, Stiles, called 'Nobby', was born at Collyhurst, Manchester, the son of an undertaker. His father and his schoolmaster, John Mulligan, recognised his talent and encouraged him to go into football. He was signed by United at fifteen, soon after he left school in 1957, gaining a regular if not undisputed place in the 1960-61 season. Although he made thirty-one League appearances for United during 1962-63, Crerand and Setters were preferred in the Cup Final team. It was not until 1963-64 that Stiles truly established himself.

Nobby was so short-sighted that he could barely recognise people at ten yards, and it was said, half-seriously, that 'he didn't tackle people, he collided with them'.

Stiles went to great lengths to pretend his eyesight was satisfactory, but one day, so the story goes, Busby discovered him reading a newspaper upside down and the truth came out. He persuaded Stiles to wear contact lenses—which improved his confidence without making a significant difference to his tackling.

Yet United's players have nothing but admiration for him. Foulkes said he had 'always had faith in his footballing ability. Nobby is an honest fellow, and a quiet man off the field, but on it he is probably one of the hardest men a forward can possibly face. He just smothers his opponent out of the game. He goes in very hard, but he has far more ability than he is given credit for, and a very good football brain.'

Stiles is not a dirty player, but a frighteningly hard one. He plays the ball, but as one England international once complained, 'it is like being tackled by a small steamroller'. To the Continental, Stiles is an anathema, essentially physical and unsophisticated, which may explain the unpardonable campaign built up against him in their press and even on their terraces. To Manchester United and later to England, remembering his performances in both World and European Cups, he has proved irreplaceable. His capacity for hard work, his religious following of instructions, his demonic running and covering, all have demoralising effect on the opposition. England might have won the World Cup without Bobby Charlton: they would not have won it without Stiles. To see him at Wembley with the Cup, socks down and toothless grin, was to see the triumph of the little man; something of a silhouette of England herself.

United, like Celtic against Inter-Milan, found they needed a player to overcome just the sort of blanket covering that Stiles could provide—someone whose flair and skill could create an opening whatever the weight of numbers, who could put pressure on an opponent and a system until they fell apart together. But when George Best arrived from Belfast's Cregagh Estate in 1962, at the age of fifteen, to use Busby's words: 'he could have walked under the table in my office'. Spindly-legged, about 5ft 6in tall, Best did not exactly look a footballer. Two Irish clubs had already decided he was too small. But United's scout, Bob Bishop, recommended to watch Best by the leader of his local youth club, had eyes only for his marvellous ball control.

Manchester almost lost Best, because when he came over for a trial, his companion, another Irish boy, took an instant dislike to the city and asked to go home the very next day. Best was so shy that he did not want to stay on his own. His father, a Belfast shipyard worker, was furious to see him back; for he had allowed Best to leave a grammar school that played rugby for a secondary school that played soccer. He immediately phoned Busby, and Best went back for another trial. It was, as Best said later, 'like a joke about the mother-in-law: I came for the day, returned for a fortnight—then I stayed for good.'

Best's return was to such effect that within a few weeks of making his first League appearance, two years later at seventeen, he was rated little short of Charlton himself. He became known as the Beatle Boy (and abroad, following El Cordobes, as El Beatle) because of his Lennon-like hairstyle. This, curiously enough, arrived by accident in the 1963-64 season. 'I was late for a Cup-tie with Barnsley and had no time to do my hair. So I merely brushed it down. It has nothing to do with the Beatles . . . I prefer the Rolling Stones, anyway.'

Best established himself after his second League appearance at Christmas, 1963. He had returned to Belfast for the holiday, but on Christmas Eve he received a telegram from Joe Armstrong asking him to report back. So he sailed on Christmas Day, helped United to beat Burnley 6-1 on Boxing Day and scored his first goal for the club.

Best, of Beatle hair and boutique wear (he has three shops in Manchester under the title 'George Best Edwardia Ltd'), is a master of extravagance. If he holds the ball too long, he can still beat player after player until only a jittery goalkeeper is left; if he delays his shot almost until the ground is rushing up to meet his ears, it will still be stretching the netting like a circus cannonball; if he lets the ball slip away, it will be back at his feet in a sudden whiplash of speed, and Best is free, like a genie out of his bottle. His secret, if genius has an element of secrecy, is the poise and balance of a ballet dancer, the power to pirouette like a spinning top; fabulous reflexes and an intense concentration on the position of the ball. There seems no antidote for the sort of poison he gives defences, as Busby once explained. 'I found with Matthews that the only way of subduing him was to cut off his source of supply—for no one can play without the ball. The same must apply to Best.'

It was often said that Best, on his day, could destroy a team with his own prodigious powers. So it would be proved, in 1965-66, when United won 5-1 on Benfica's own ground.* Busby said later, 'We planned to contain them . . . but George must have had cotton wool in his ears when we decided our tactics. Within the first quarter of an hour he had beaten them on his own with two goals

* See Chapter 11.

and another made for Connelly. It was fantastic and I was angry with him. Well, almost. . . .'

Compared to Best, John Connelly was almost an ordinary winger, and yet for a time he filled a most useful role in United's side. Born in St Helens, he was signed by Burnley from the local club in 1956 as an inside-left, then turned into a winger, fast and direct, with elusive footwork. He became an intermittent choice for England, regaining his place after Busby signed him in 1964 for £40,000. A measure of his success was the fact that Blackburn Rovers, not a rich club, were prepared to buy him from United for the same sum two years later.

Another forward who proved as good, if not better, at Old Trafford was David Herd, born at Hamilton, and son of the former Manchester City and Stockport County forward, Alex Herd. David even played alongside his father in the Stockport team after turning professional with the club in 1951. Arsenal paid £8,000 for his transfer in August, 1964, and Scotland capped him in 1959 and 1961. Busby first became interested in him when he was weighing up players for the Scottish national team, which he managed for a while before Munich. Herd, he thought, had the physique and determination to play the difficult 'front' role, in which a player spends much of his time in the opposing half with his back to the defenders. The position invites hard or foul tackling and few can fill it for long without losing some of their enthusiasm. Herd, oblivious to danger, never flinched from the task; his skills and sense of opportunity were lifted by the greater players around him.

Pat Crerand, born at Glasgow in the Gorbals, was already an established player with Celtic when Busby paid £56,000 for him in March, 1963. His ability, or his adaptability, were shown by his superb display in the Cup Final a few months later, after only a handful of first team games in his new colours. Crerand is often accused of being a one-pace player, which, in the sense that he rarely accelerates or decelerates suddenly, is certainly true. But Busby has never put much stock in speed or stamina for their own sake, important as they may be within the context of teamwork. Crerand's great asset is his reading of the game, an unusual insight into the weakness of the opposition, and how it can be exploited ruthlessly by confronting it with United's greatest strength. His passing, over any distance, has a mathematical precision, and he knows just when to release the ball to give it maximum effect. As a defender, he has his limitations; as an attacking wing-half he is like a conveyor-belt bringing ammunition to his forward-line.

Busby's biggest and most significant transfer was that of Denis Law, who cost almost £115,000 from Torino in the 1962 close season. Born in Aberdeen, Law was missed by his local club, but in view of his physical appearance, this was scarcely surprising. Archie Beattie, brother of Huddersfield's manager and the club's northern scout, sent Law south for a trial on the strength of his performances for Bowis Secondary Modern. Andy Beattie thought his brother was pulling his leg, for Law measured 5ft 3in, weighted 8st 9lb, had an ugly boil on his cheek and wore spectacles to correct a squint.

But an eye operation and a judicious diet of steak put Law into shape for first-class football. He made his first appearance on Christmas Eve, 1956, against Notts County, when he was sixteen years, 303 days—the beginning of an astonishing rise to the top. In March, 1960,

Manchester City bought him for £53,000, and sold him to Torino for more than £100,000 in June, 1961, when transfers to Italy were all the rage.

Law, single and impetuous, rebelled against the rigid discipline that reigned as much at Torino as at Greaves' Milan. He was bored by the lack of familiar entertainment, pestered by the press, manipulated like a puppet by his Italian masters. He spent some of his money on a Jaguar, which was involved in an accident, putting Law and his Scottish team mate, Joe Baker, in hospital. Hardly had this trouble subsided, when Law was sent off the field during a Cup-tie against Napoli . . . by his own coach, Beniamino Santos, for taking a throw-in contrary to instructions. At the end of the season Torino transferred him back to England, and there were angry demonstrations by their supporters outside the club offices.

The campaign in Italy nevertheless added a new edge, a new dimension to his game, creating the unparalleled fusion of thought and movement that makes Law so prodigal a player when fit and well. After Di Stefano, he has become possibly the finest striker in European football, able to make an immense contribution to attack and defence should the need arise. As a spearhead he possesses formidable powers—exquisite ball control, rapid acceleration, marvellous accuracy; the ability to move faster and to jump higher than an opponent at any given moment. Foulkes thought that his suspensions were explained by his dislike of being beaten: 'he gets into trouble so frequently because he tries to retrieve the ball quickly when beaten in a tackle. He can take chances that would not be chances at all to inferior players. His reflexes are out of this world.'

The new United were completed by a permutation of goalkeepers, Pat Dunne or Gregg or Gaskell; by Foulkes, playing on week after week with a painful Achilles tendon injury because there was no one to take his place; and by Bobby Charlton, in grace and character the greatest of all.

You're not . . .

10

Bobby Charlton

His family tree made it almost inevitable that Robert Charlton would be a footballer. Four generations on his mother's side had kicked a ball in earnest, first for the little mining village of Ashington, Northumberland, and later for county or League sides. Charlton's mother Cissie, was a Milburn, a famous name in football history. His great-great-grandfather, Jack Milburn, was a fearsome player who appeared regularly for Northumberland in the late 1880's. His son, also Jack (but known mysteriously as 'Tanner') played in goal for Ashington, and had the peculiar distinction of being so left-handed that he even used his left when diving towards the right. Between matches for Ashington, who were struggling in the lower reaches of the Football League, Jack trained professional sprinters; he also found time to have six sons and five daughters, who all played football . . . even the girls, one of whom, according to Jack, ought to have been England's centre-forward! The boys turned professional; Jack, George and Jimmy with Leeds United, Stan with Leicester City. Jack and George were left- and right-back at Leeds in the days of Wilf Copping; even the goal-keeper, Harry Potts, was their father's brother-in-law. George eventually went to Chesterfield, where he became trainer; brother Jimmy took over at full-back. Bobby's brother, Jackie, also went to Leeds in 1952, where he became centre-half. As Jackie put it: 'For a long time we've been keeping them in players and they've been keeping us in ha'pence.'

Bobby recalls that he never saw his uncles play 'except in the street at Ashington. They would come home from a match and, with about five minutes of their coming through the door, the house would be turned upside down. About five minutes more after that the lot of us—me, them and half the kids in Ashington—would be in the street chasing a ball about.'

But by far the best of the Milburns was his mother's cousin, 'Wor' Jackie, who became the idol of Newcastle. His speed, dynamism and shooting power (he scored 178 goals in League games) put him among the best players in England, for whom he played thirteen times. Here, indeed, were some of the inherent qualities that Charlton was to reveal at an even more spectacular level.

Charlton's father took an interest in Bobby's progress, but was never a fan. 'At first,' said Charlton, half-seriously, 'he would have been hard put to tell the difference between a football and a pomegranate. He married football when he married mother. But the technicalities of it have always been over his head.'

Mr Charlton's principal role in the early days was to deal with one talent scout in the parlour while Mrs Charlton entertained another in the drawing-room—sometimes from the same teapot. But Manchester United got in first, being tipped off by Bobby's schoolmaster even before he had a schoolboy trial. Charlton thought 'this early interest of United's gave them a head start. It left me with a soft spot for them.'

So the schoolboy international who had scored two

goals at Wembley from inside-left went to Manchester, where he found himself in a hostel with a dozen or so other United players. Not just youngsters, but first-team men like Blanchflower, Jones and Edwards—part of Busby's scheme to mould a vibrant team spirit.

Charlton spent some of his time learning to be an engineer as both Busby and his mother were keen for him to have a proper trade. 'There was no apprentice-professional scheme in those days and the ground staff boys spent much of their time sweeping the ground or cleaning the lavatories. That wasn't my mother's idea of how to earn a living, so I promised her I would take a second job in case I flopped as a footballer.

'Every morning as I left the house at seven, Duncan [Edwards] would call "Don't slam the door". He had another two hours in bed. If making the grade meant staying in bed longer, I was going to make the grade.'

There was, at this time, a certain laziness in Charlton's psychology and a built-in resistance to routine. He did not take easily to training for its own sake, preferring to kick a ball around than go through the grind. He seemed to take it for granted that he would get into the first team on natural talent rather than by painstaking effort. He was perhaps more prominent off the field than on it in Manchester, spending a lot of his spare time in dance-halls and cinemas, obsessed by pop-records and, strangely, also by fishing.

Charlton turned professional in 1955, soon after his seventeenth birthday—he was born in October, 1938—but did not play in League football for another year. Even then Busby only picked him because he was in trouble through injuries. Charlton recalls that he 'got into the side on false pretences—saying I was fit when I wasn't. The Boss asked me if I was okay, which was a silly question really, because I was bound to say yes. In fact my right ankle was swollen like a balloon after playing against Manchester City reserves the previous Saturday. We were playing Charlton in London, and I scored two goals with my left foot; I was a natural right-footer, but with that injury it was strictly for standing on.'

But Charlton was still a reserve, and ten goals in fourteen matches during 1956-57 scarcely made him a national hero. It was only in the two months before Munich that Charlton began to respond favourably to the pressures of first-team football, scoring two superb goals to take United through to the semi-final at the expense of Red Star Belgrade.

The disaster left him with scars more psychological than physical. 'I wasn't hurt. I wasn't even deeply troubled in my mind. I just couldn't take it in, and therefore it washed over me. I didn't want to accept what had happened.'

When Charlton came back to reality, the spectators did not. They identified themselves with the survivor, who had only to play well to appear to play brilliantly. Charlton had been in just as promising form before Munich, but now he knew that to get the results that sentiment demanded the team had to show more energy. 'I gave everything I had and I stayed in a match the whole ninety minutes, even if it meant rushing about looking for the ball when my legs felt like water. I knew I had to do that, the same as the other players knew they had to do it if we were to get by.'

Also, the timing of Charlton's greatest moments, accidental or not, was immaculate. The maze-like run against West Bromwich, the explosive shots against Fulham, the

stepney

UNITED '68

brennan

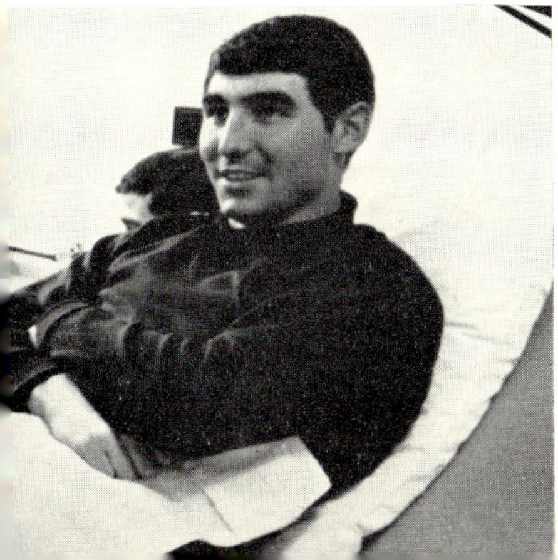

dunne

stiles

crerand

foulkes

sadler

kidd

aston

herd

burns

law

fitzpatrick

best

charlton

striking of Hopkinson's post at Wembley; then, as he became a national figure, the unbelievable volleyed goal against Scotland at Hampden Park—still perhaps the greatest Charlton has scored—and two more thunderbolts to save England's face against Portugal.

But this artificial impetus had to fade. Charlton was changed by the responsibilities that Munich forced on him, but only from one form of instability to another. Where he had been exuberant, now he was moody; where he had been nervous, now he was nerveless—or, more accurately, constricted emotionally so that a calm exterior hid the conflicting sensations within him. By forcing his game to an unnatural tempo, he so drained himself physically and mentally that a relapse was inevitable. It came when playing for England in Belgrade, an unbearable place for him to return to; Charlton had an appalling match, and in spite of increasing pressure the selectors ignored him for the 1958 World Cup.

The next few years marked the time of Charlton the individual, exciting but unpredictable, and of questionable value to his team. Even when he formed with Viollet and Quixall the most formidable inside trio in England, he would still run obsessively with the ball, creating movement for his own sake, as though to satisfy some artistic craving within him. England recalled him, and persevered because of his moments of genius—the superb swivel, acceleration and shot which brought a goal against Italy in 1959, the soaring header that beat Scotland at Wembley. Walter Winterbottom eventually stuck him at outside-left on the summer tour, and Busby, who was equally short of a left-winger, followed suit; the results were pleasing, if not entirely satisfactory.

Charlton hated the left wing, but it was better than

being dropped, as he had been even by United in the 1959-60 season. He tended to drift inside looking for the ball, which irritated his colleagues and unbalanced the team. Worse, it tended to encourage his spasmodic talents of dribbling and speculative shooting. On a good day Charlton was irresistible; on a bad one, which came when the mood took him, he missed greatness by a long distance. Even his consistent and superb form as England's left-winger during the 1962 World Cup, when he was named in the 'select' team of the tournament, was followed by a hernia operation, convalescence, and yet more inconsistency.

Somewhere around this time, it is difficult to pinpoint a date, Charlton came to terms with himself. He realised, as he said, that he was not 'an intelligent player in the football sense, like Danny Blanchflower or Dennis Viollet. The solution,' he concluded, was 'further experience in a more demanding role.' Marriage at twenty-three to Norma, a former fashion model, in July 1961, brought unexpected maturity. The responsibilities of family life—he now has two daughters—created a different, less retiring Charlton. He became less of an individual, more of a team player, showing that he could start and continue a movement as often and expertly as he finished them. For the first time he worked hard at passing, which became as accurate and as positively ambitious as any in the League. Sir Alf Ramsey appreciated his new, more complex role for United, and he moulded the England team around it; until, in the 1966 World Cup, when he played as a withdrawn centre-forward, Charlton's dual talents as schemer and finisher received their fullest expression.

Charlton has at last achieved the consistency inseparable from true greatness. He is mature, vastly experienced, able to see the vulnerable points and to direct his shafts against them. He rarely has a bad game, and the moments of brilliance have been moulded into the work of the team. But it is still the goals that leave their biggest impact. When the blond figure with thinning hair comes on the ball an electric impulse of anticipatory excitement surges through the crowd, a hum of sound rising to a roar. A little tap, and Charlton's extravagant gifts come into play, the deceptive, accelerating pace, the natural, sinuous swerve, rarely disguised but so swift and stunning that prior knowledge is not enough to frustrate it. The defence goes one way, on a lumbering hinge, and Charlton, turning acutely and sensationally in his tracks, goes the other. The goal may be thirty yards distant, the goalkeeper may be flexed and prepared; but he is faced by a player who can shoot harder and more accurately than any man alive; so the ball becomes a blur and is suddenly straining the meshes of his net, behind or even before his fruitless acrobatics. Charlton turns away, and the eruptive volcano is silent, leaving a trail of destruction in its wake. The dazzling skill stays in the mind's eye, like some landscape lit by a flash of lightning on a stormy night.

11

Europe: So Near and yet so Far

If, in the last analysis, Manchester United depended on Charlton for the true inspiration, a flick from the sorcerer's wand, much of the new team had become moulded together. Pat Dunne, a sharp and courageous if not dominating goalkeeper; Brennan and Tony Dunne, two fast and reliable full-backs, formed Eire's last trio of defence as well as United's. Stiles had established himself as the defensive wing-half, a pillar of support for Foulkes, immensely mobile and indefatigable. Crerand and Charlton linked in midfield, providing the service for two formidable wingers in Connelly and Best, the discovery of the 1964-65 season. Herd, the tip of United's spear, took some of the weight off Law, better suited to sudden, stunning advances than an exposed, expectant wait in the penalty area.

Yet United were prone to fall between the proverbial stools—appropriately a three-legged seat, with League, Cup and Fairs' Cup all in contention. United made a good start in the First Division, gaining a rare point in a 3-3 draw at Everton, and beating the champions, Liverpool, 2-0. Yet they were always breathlessly pursuing the fanatically fit young men of Chelsea and the durable and dour players of Leeds United, newly promoted. If any team seemed likely to crack it was Manchester, who acquired a disheartening knack of playing their opponents to a standstill yet squandering one or two points in a moment of carelessness or inept finishing. Birmingham City, fielding so many defenders that their penalty area looked like Piccadilly Circus during the rush hour, Sheffield United and West Bromwich Albion all scrambled outrageous draws at Old Trafford; and Fulham, as was their wont, actually won at Craven Cottage as part of their annual surpassing of Houdini. Law, too, was sent off at Blackpool and suspended for a month, including the vital Christmas fixtures.

The penalty of success, a compound of exacting matches, began to tell. Although United knocked a little wind out of Chelsea's sails with a 4-0 win at Old Trafford, they were beaten 1-0 at home by Leeds, who actually played well enough to deserve it. Even when United reached the last four of the F.A. Cup, eliminating Chester, Stoke City, Burnley and Wolves, their form grew worse, not better. A week before the semi-final they played dreadfully at Sheffield Wednesday, who won 1-0. Foulkes, with grim humour, said that he 'made Wednesday's centre-forward, John Hickton, look like Alfredo Di Stefano.'

Sure enough, Leeds got a draw on the same ground the following Saturday in a disgraceful brawl for which the referee, timid and indecisive, must take some of the blame. Bremner scored from Collins' free-kick to win the replay, which a different referee handled better before he was knocked out by a young spectator as he left the field. These matches were unhappy symptoms of a double malaise among all Manchester's dazzling endeavour: too many of their players bore a smouldering fuse lit too easily by the high stakes and emotion; they respected

Busby's high demands of discipline, but unlike the Babes, there were moments when they chose to forget them. The supporters, too, frenetic and faithful to the last, had become a gregarious menace—an ominous secular arm of an almost religious cause.

The press wrote off United for a second year, but this only spurred them to exceptional efforts. After losing to Leeds in the Cup they won 5-0 against Blackburn Rovers at Ewood Park, where Charlton, moving from the depths to the heights, scored a true and brilliant hat-trick. Then came the critical away match at Leeds, which was expected to be decisive for the title. Busby told United they had to win, that they might as well lose as draw; he decided to start the match with five orthodox forwards, even Charlton forsaking his deep role in midfield. With a gale at their backs, United made half-a-dozen chances before Leeds could catch their breath; and after fourteen minutes Connelly scored a good goal. Leeds' control was inept in the difficult conditions, and even in the second half one would have thought the wind was against them instead of being in their favour. Charlton moved back, and with Stiles apparently clairvoyant, United held on to win. Thereafter, with Chelsea's morale collapsing after Docherty sent most of the team home from Blackpool, United held their advantage. They expected to need a point in their last match, at Villa Park, but while they were beating Arsenal 2-1 Leeds fell 3-0 behind against the bottom club, Birmingham, and the draw they eventually got was not enough. Enjoying a vastly superior goal average, United could afford to lose to Aston Villa; which, with typical thoroughness, they did.

United took their first European Cup-tie against HIJ

Helsinki a little too easily, winning only 3-2 away, after Herd and Connelly had scored in the first fifteen minutes. The absence of Crerand, replaced by the inexperienced John Fitzpatrick, left them firing on only three cylinders. Although Law scored an opportunist goal and United led 3-1 at half-time, HIJ were never overawed by the reputation of their opponents. Peltionemi reduced the lead to a single goal, and the sleek Manchester defence looked a little dishevelled in the closing minutes. Busby was not pleased by the performance; United had been too indifferent in a competition where no team, not even the Finnish amateurs, are completely outclassed.

Crerand returned for the second leg, as did Best, whom Busby moved to inside forward, giving a run to John Aston on the left-wing. Aston, whose father had played for United's outstanding post-war team, showed some deft touches but inevitably drew an unfavourable comparison with Best himself. Not that United were in any sense troubled. Two goals up at half-time, they eventually won 6-0, Connelly scoring three goals, Best (2) and Charlton the others. The sweating Heinonen, always exhorting his defence to fresh efforts, did a lot to keep the score below double figures.

Pat Dunne also replaced Gaskell, but he was unfit to play in United's next tie, against the East German champions, Vorwärts Berlin. This gave a fresh chance to Gregg, who had been languishing in United's second or third team for the best part of a year. The combined shock of the air disaster and the delayed effects of the injury received in the 1958 Cup Final had left him far from fit, and it was not until early in the 1965-66 season that he regained his best form, after missing the Cup and League medals won by United. His return delighted everyone at Old Trafford, for Gregg had never been a lucky goalkeeper. When a teenager with Linfield he broke a wrist so seriously that doctors feared he would not be able to use the hand properly again, let alone keep goal. Then, at Doncaster, he broke two bones in his arm in a collision with the Blackburn centre-forward. Even a harmless kickabout in Ireland during the next close-season resulted in a broken ankle.

Gregg played outstandingly in the drab People's Stadium at East Berlin, and his confidence spread through the whole defence. After a difficult first half, in which Manchester struggled against the unequal combination of a freezing temperature and a frozen ground, the game turned sharply in their favour. Vorwärts' lack of control cost them far more energy in fruitless chasing and retrieving, their stamina began to fade, and in the last twenty minutes they fell irretrievably behind. United poured out of defence, Charlton reached Herd on the wing, and Vorwärts seemed unperturbed by his high centre, which seemed certain to drop harmlessly into the hands of the waiting Weiss. But Law, escaping Unger's clutches, hovered above him like a stalling bird and headed a phenomenal goal. Then, in another riposte, he drew Weiss out with delightful footwork and pulled his pass out of reach for Connelly to score easily.

Dunne replaced Gregg for the second leg—it was not clear whether injury or status was decisive—which fortunately United were able to play at Old Trafford, the East Germans for once receiving visas to enter a N.A.T.O. country. Manchester quickly consolidated their advantage when Stiles scampered around Kalinke's legs like a terrier, and Law pulled his pass in front of the advancing Herd, whose shot was too powerful for Vorwärts' reserve goalkeeper, Zulkowski. The match became more even, and consequently more interesting, as Vorwärts abandoned all pretence of defence in an attempt to salvage the situation. Frässdorf left the crossbar trembling above Dunne's head, but Law, with another astonishingly acrobatic header, caused similar vibrations on the opposite woodwork. Vorwärts could find no fair means of keeping the ball away from Law in the air, and when he beat Unger close to goal, Herd hit an instantancous shot into the net. Vorwärts offered a suspicion of a revival after half-time, scoring splendidly through Piepenburg, the credit going mainly to Begerad, who bisected two defenders with a marvellous pass. But Herd, whose finishing was above criticism in this match, soon popped up for his third, completing a devious move between Connelly and Law. United, indeed, could always raise their game to a level beyond the Germans' range of vision, concealing science with artistry, altogether a higher dimension of football.

The mediocrity of Vorwärts departed: the glamour of Benfica arrived, They had recalled Bela Guttmann as manager, a popular choice, judging by the huge crowd that turned out to welcome him at Lisbon airport. But his old genius seemed to be missing. Benfica trailed behind Sporting in the League, and Guttmann used ten reserves in a European tie against Stade Dudelange of Luxembourg, because the first team had not tried hard enough in a prestige friendly with Rangers. Too much depended on Eusebio, who pulled Benfica through the next round against Levski almost on his own, overshadowing even the renowned Bulgarian centre-forward, Asparoukhov.

At Old Trafford Benfica were almost beaten to their

knees, but when the ball ran well for them their old confidence returned; their hidden reserves of strength surprised United, and all but took them out of a vibrating tie. The Stretford End bellowed its titanic roar after only five minutes, when Herd headed Best's free-kick hard against Pereira's post; but Benfica were soon in front, Augusto, lamentably unguarded, needing only to sidefoot Eusebio's ingeniously curving corner. Then United put on the pressure, Stiles, Law and Best combined beautifully, and Best's final pass, timed to the split second, put Herd clean through for the equaliser. As Crerand and Stiles took control in midfield the options for the attack mounted; Benfica's flagging defenders, fighting for breath, held off the tackle dangerously close to their own penalty area. Charlton, sensing space behind him, pivoted dramatically, hooked the ball across with his left foot for Law, with lightning reactions, to score before Pereira could lift a finger.

Foulkes, coming up for the set-pieces, met Cantwell's floating free-kick perfectly on the hour, although Pereira should surely have stopped it. United showed more confidence in Gregg, perhaps too much, for Eusebio left him helpless with three shots from thirty yards that skimmed past the post and all but decapitated some spectators. Gregg, re-established in United's first team, was slow to move to Eusebio's best centre, imparted with cunning spin from the outside of the boot, curving right to Torres' feet only yards from goal. Three-two, and United's lead was uncomfortably narrow, with Eusebio holding the balance. Only in the last ten minutes did the Portuguese show signs of distress, but United could not quite find the final touch. Even when Law headed Connelly's superb centre goalwards from five yards Costa Pereira deflected the ball with instinctive fingertips on to the bar. Law, rising skywards again, returned it to the horizontal for a second and fruitless rebound. Benfica's goal, in English eyes, bore a charmed life indeed.

Manchester travelled to Lisbon with misgivings. Here the Portuguese were another team, capable of attacking football that could destroy everything in its path. They had succeeded Real Madrid as the most formidable and frightening opposition to confront on their own ground. Since 1960 they had played eighteen home matches in the European Cup and won them all, scoring seventy-eight goals and conceding only thirteen. Only twice had Benfica failed to score at least three goals and only twice had they conceded more than one; fifteen of their victories had a margin of at least two goals, some of them many more. Among their victims were Ujpest of Hungary (6-2), Rapid Vienna (3-0), FK Austria (5-1), Nuremberg (6-0), Tottenham (3-1), Norrkoping (5-1), Vasas Gyor (4-0). Even Real Madrid, still among the best teams in Europe, had been crushed 5-1 on their last visit in the previous season. Statistics as long and staggering as these could not lie.

Yet like many teams before, the certainty of victory was Benfica's Achilles heel. So concerned were they with attack, that the possibility of defeat, of conceding an early goal, did not enter their heads. Best, scorning defence, started an early offensive, but even he could not have dreamed of its devastating effect. Germano and the declining Costa Pereira made surprising mistakes, and United were on them in a flash, making every bullet count. After six minutes Charlton was brought down, Tony Dunne took the free-kick, and Best timed his leap to the inch and the moment. After twelve Gregg punted high down the middle, Herd's flicked header, downwards and backwards, took Germano out of play, and Best weaved round three astounded defenders all on his own for a sensational goal. After fifteen Charlton, Law and Connelly created a huge gap with an impudent triangle of tricks, leaving Connelly to smash the ball home from point-blank range. No one could believe their eyes: Benfica, again leading the Portuguese League, had geared themselves to topple the impudent British; instead, they were dazzled by a reflection of their own impending whirlwind.

United momentarily lost their poise when Brennan (replacing Cantwell) decided to lob back to Gregg and, in the mood of the moment, flicked the ball nonchalantly without looking; unfortunately Gregg had advanced for an interception, so the lob sailed straight over his head. But Benfica still played without conviction, and Stiles tackled Eusebio with increasing confidence and decreasing ferocity. In the final minutes Manchester pulled out of sight, Law putting Crerand through for a fourth, then Charlton, in unstoppable form, swerving past three defenders for the final, humiliating touch. To win by five goals to one, and that an own goal, where no club had even drawn before was an unforgettable, prodigious performance. On this night in Lisbon United were at the very peak of their potential, producing a breathtaking display of football that would have reduced any team to a shaking ruin.

But in that paradoxical manner of Manchester United, their brilliance deserted them as quickly as it had come. Poor performances in the League meant that their title rested between Liverpool and Leeds, with Liverpool running away at the finish. By the time of the European

Cup semi-final, United knew they had to win the trophy to stay in the competition; and yet self-confidence abounded out of all proportion. Their opponents, Partizan Belgrade, were not a great team, but a good one. They included seven internationals, among them Jusufi, a superb full-back; Galic, arguably Europe's best centre-forward; Vasovic, making giant strides forwards in defence; and Soskic, second only to Yashin over the past five years. Partizan had disposed of Nantes, Werder Bremen and Sparta Prague, whom they beat 5-0 in Belgrade after losing 4-1 in Czechoslovakia.

United should have been warned by Partizan's remarkable recovery, but they played carelessly and incompetently in Belgrade, wasting any number of chances in the first half-hour. Law, six yards out, tried to burst the netting and instead almost splintered the crossbar. The ball spun back with such violence that Herd, whose gifts never lay in dexterity of footwork, got it into a shooting position with as much ease as a mechanical shovel. He fiddled so long that Becejac, who had been lying injured on the ground, decided that after all it was worth recovering, and cleared. Then Best, whom Busby had ill-advisedly risked in spite of a bad leg injury received in a recent League match, broke down completely. Substitutes were still an option of the future, so he had to stay on, aggravating the injury to such an extent that he was to miss the return. With Best a passenger, Partizan took over the match. Gregg committed himself to a cross from Jusufi, a rash move, but understandable when Foulkes and Brennan were so uncertain in the air. At any rate, Hasanagic beat everyone to the ball, and with the net quite unoccupied, had only to head it straight to score. A few minutes later Becejac scored from an unexpectedly accurate pass by Vasovic, leaving United in trouble.

In the second leg we saw a different, realistic Partizan, wholly committed to holding their advantage. Busby, troubled by injuries, introduced Anderson on the right-wing; he was inevitably rather out of his depth in a match of such high tension and critical importance. United, lacking Best to winkle out openings, found Partizan a reluctant snail when it came to the feast. After seventy-five minutes of fruitless bombardment, mainly from long range or culminating in fruitless, unimaginative centres, Stiles at last got himself and the ball down to the by-line. Soskic left his mark for the presumed cross a fraction too soon, and Stiles hit the ball in off his body from the acutest possible angle. Partizan momentarily lost their composure, but when Charlton, seizing a half-chance through tireless activity, smashed a tremendous volley inches over the bar, United knew that a play-off had eluded them. Law and Charlton could have saved the tie at their best; but on the day, United huffed and puffed without much hope of blowing down Soskic's wall.

For Busby, this was a time for agonising reappraisal. Partizan went on to lose to Real Madrid in the final, but neither of these teams, nor even the declining Inter-Milan, were equal to United at their best. The truth, possibly unpalatable, was that his team, allowed too much to play by ear, lacked the organisation that might have made better use of their brilliant potential. In particular, the risks of attacking football, when advocated without regard for the circumstances, were greater than the rewards. In the future, perhaps by tacit understanding rather than by radical instructions, United were prepared to exploit others' energy and conserve their own; to hold by strategy what they had gained by skill.

12

Europe: The Edge of Triumph

With Charlton consistently good, and Law quite brilliant, Manchester United regained the League championship in emphatic fashion. They survived a traumatic home defeat by Norwich City in the third round of the F.A. Cup, and the loss of Herd, who broke a leg against Leicester City in March, 1967, to outdistance Nottingham Forest in the home straight. United made certain of the title by winning 6-1 at West Ham, the sort of élan that promised greater triumphs in Europe.

Perhaps the most significant change in the team was in goal, where Alex Stepney joined United for £55,000 in September, 1966. Chelsea had signed him during the close season to cover the rumoured departure of Peter Bonetti; but Bonetti stayed, and Stepney moved on, after making only one first-team appearance for the London club.

Born in Mitcham, London, Stepney joined Millwall, his first professional club, in May, 1963, succeeding Beswick as first-team goalkeeper at the start of the following season. By 1966 he had emerged as the best goalkeeper in the Second Division, and among the best in the country.

Busby said candidly: 'I don't think we would have won the championship without Stepney.' Foulkes supported his view. 'Stepney,' he observed, 'is not just a very good goalkeeper. He stays cool and composed even when he has made a mistake. You know where you are with him, you can work something out with a fellow like that.'

Stepney agreed that he 'had never been a flashy goalkeeper. What matters to me,' he said, 'is the record of goals scored against me. What I want to see is forty-two games played and no more than forty-two goals scored against. That way I am happy.

'Certainly I was nervous at first, but that was because I was suddenly with the most famous team in the country and I did not know anyone. Now I know what the defence is going to do and they know what I am going to do.'

Stepney, so composed in a crisis, has extraordinary reactions, agility and handling ability. His only weakness has been a tendency to remain on the line, or, worse still, to commit himself prematurely to an excessive advance. But such errors have become less apparent, particularly since he joined the England party for training under Sir Alf Ramsey.

After Connelly's departure to Blackburn, Best moved to the right wing, allowing Busby ultimately to settle for John Aston on the left. Aston, born in Manchester, began very much as the son of his father, right back for United in the first great team immediately after the war. An unassuming, unspectacular player, the junior Aston attracted attention mainly when he made mistakes. There was, and is, a deceptive, almost irrelevant manner about his style, so that even the most remarkable footwork or movement can pass almost unnoticed. For a long time Aston was harshly criticised by United's supporters, abuse which he bore stoically, even though it must have affected him. The less discerning critics did not appreciate how he scarcely wasted a ball; if he had none of the consuming fantasy of Best, he had none of his irritating excesses either. Aston's contribution to teamwork has been immense in terms of goals scored from his efforts. He was to play his greatest match for United in the European Cup Final, and no one could ask for more than that.

Busby, however, still had room for someone who could function anywhere. The most versatile of his new discoveries was David Sadler, born in Yalding in Kent, and who played for Maidstone United while working in a bank; he became one of the youngest to win an England amateur cap. United won the race for his signature in November, 1962, and persuaded him to turn professional in the following February. Maidstone had used him as an inside-forward, and it was at centre-forward, replacing Herd, that Sadler made his debut in the first team. He had twelve successive matches, received excessive publicity, and lost his place. Thereafter he made only rare appearances for two years, until, in 1965-66, he became a regular choice, not establishing himself in any one position but playing well in several. Busby at first saw him as a replacement for Foulkes, and England gave him a full cap at centre-half against Ireland in October, 1967. But Foulkes arrested his decline, and as Sadler revealed disquieting shortcomings in the air, a place was often found for both of them. His best role proved to be in midfield, where he shone neither as provider or finisher, yet had prodigious stamina and an uncanny knack of appearing in the right place at the right time.

United used their Australasian tour to blood three more

players—Jimmy Rimmer, now ahead of Gregg, Gaskell and Pat Dunne in the goalkeeping hierarchy; Francis Burns, whose promise at wing-half was temporarily cut short by a knee injury that required a cartilage operation; and Brian Kidd, a new prodigy. Kidd, son of a Manchester bus driver, had a remarkable tour at inside-forward, prompting Jack Crompton to call him 'A revelation; he matures with every game.' Barely eighteen—he was born in May, 1949—Kidd was brought up in the cobbled streets of Collyhurst, a Manchester suburb. 'We used the arches of a warehouse for goals; the streetlights used to light the place up and we would play until all hours.' When Kidd was with Manchester Boys, Joe Armstrong spotted him and signed him on schoolboy forms. A modest boy, subdued and unsure of himself, Kidd wanted to leave United for another club because he was rather overawed by the weight of talent around him. 'Mr Busby told me I could get nowhere in life without working hard, and that I must have confidence in myself.' So he stayed, went in the youth team, then had two seasons in the reserves—he was top scorer in 1966-67—before he made the grade.

In sharp contrast to the holders, Celtic, United had the easiest possible draw in the first round of the European Cup—against the Maltese champions, Hibernian. Managed by Father Hilary Tagliaferro, a priest who sat on the touchline in his full habit, the Maltese put up a brave fight at Old Trafford and could even have won the rather academic return. While United's only problem was Law, who played with a bruised toe, Hibernian's seventeen-year-old left-winger, Francis Mifsud, got lost in London for two days and only turned up just in time to play. Law and Sadler duly scored two goals each, the first after twelve minutes, and the ball bobbed continuously around the Maltese penalty area; but Privitera, Carvana and Mallia defended vigorously, and only Best's exciting skills made a real impact in a mediocre match.

United showed little inclination to exert themselves in the second leg on a bumpy pitch in steaming conditions. Dunne hit the post with a free-kick after sixteen minutes, but Hibernian, packing their defence, kept the game if not the tie alive. Stiles had a scuffle with Privitera to liven the second half; Best hit the post; then Charlton nearly dislodged the crossbar with a shot from close range. Yet with Mizzi in superb form, Hibernian held out, and had a fine chance to embarrass the English champions after sixty-eight minutes, when Zerri hit the ball well wide of Stepney, who turned his shot round the post in a flurry of acrobatics. After this escape the game petered out as a goalless draw.

United showed more positive form in the League, establishing a lead and putting the rising Manchester City in their place with a 2-1 win at Maine Road. City scored first through Colin Bell, but Stepney brilliantly stopped everything else; Charlton scored twice and Best had a sensational match. But the good news that Kidd had been chosen for the England Under-23 team was offset by another suspension for Law, sent off against Arsenal on October 7. This time it was six weeks, and although Busby tried to have him released for the next European Cup tie against Sarajevo, the F.A. would have none of it.

The problem of resources accumulated when Stiles, who had injured a knee against Sheffield United, failed to respond to treatment over a three week period. Doctors advised a cartilage operation, putting him out of action for a further six weeks. With Herd still in convalescence, and Brennan also out of sorts, Busby turned in the crisis to Burns and John Fitzpatrick. Burns, a Scottish youth international, disguised his inexperience expertly throughout United's European Cup campaign, playing both at full-back and in midfield; he was desperately unlucky not to win a place in the final. Fitzpatrick, another Scot, from Aberdeen, had longer hair even than Best; he filled Stiles' role with dogged endeavour.

Yet United were more than glad to draw the first leg in Yugoslavia, reaching Sarajevo after an arduous journey on the winding road from Dubrovnik Airport. FK Sarajevo had no previous experience in the European Cup, but their team looked formidable with its four internationals, including right-back Fazlagic, the national captain. Musemic, appearing in his first match since an appendix operation one month earlier, had United in trouble after twenty-one minutes. He left Foulkes groping and shot wide of Stepney, who slowed his shot but could not stop it; the ball seemed to cross the line before Stepney recovered, but the referee was unsighted and refused to allow a goal. To add injury to insult Sarajevo's outside-right, Prodanovic, who had been scolded by the referee for his violent protests, was hurt in a tackle and went off the field; he took no further part. As the match simmered along barely under control, fists and boots flew. Crerand ironically said later that 'Jack Crompton, our trainer, was on the field so much I bet half the crowd thought he was playing.' While United played unashamedly for a draw, Kidd came closest to a goal with a shot to the top corner which Mustic deflected at fullest stretch.

Fitzpatrick was unable to play in the return because

of a suspension following a caution in a Central League match against Liverpool Reserves; so Burns moved into midfield and Brennan regained his place at full-back. Sarajevo were also below full strength, for Prodanovic's injury proved serious enough to keep him out for six months at least.

United dictated the early part of the match, with Crerand, in great form, setting up attack after attack. Kidd hit the post from twenty-five yards and after eleven minutes Brennan and Crerand spurted out of defence to start another fine move. Kidd, finding plenty of time and space, produced a measured centre for Best; Mustic parried his header at full stretch and Aston, instantly alert, ran in to score just inside the post.

Although United had a momentary scare when Stepney barely got a hand to a fierce shot from Antic just after half-time, Best immediately quivered a post, forced a breathtaking save out of Mustic, then hit the post again. The tension could almost be cut with a knife when Best became involved in an incident with Mustic which escaped the referee. Mustic complained to his colleagues that he had been struck in the face and Prljaca seized the first opportunity that presented itself for a tackle of such violence on Best that the sending off was inevitable.

All Sarajevo's grievances became still more magnified by United's second goal, scored by Best from a reverse pass, which seemed unmistakably over the by-line. Sarajevo, to their credit, remained unshaken by this second serious miscarriage of justice. Stepney had to make another blinding save from Antic, and when Delalic headed in a cross from Blazevic, United were reminded uncomfortably that another lapse, on the away goals rule, would put them out of the Cup. But only three minutes remained and Sarajevo, try as they could, were frustrated to the finish.

As December crept into January another United player went on the injured list—Foulkes, with torn knee fibres. He failed a fitness test when United were taken to an F.A. Cup replay by the holders, Tottenham Hotspur, and beaten 1-0 at White Hart Lane. Herd, at least, was back; but he clearly needed time to rediscover the pace of First Division football.

And of the European Cup. As the competitors diminished, the competition intensified. United's opponents in the quarter-final were Gornik Zabrze, the Polish champions who had disposed of Dynamo Kiev, no less, the conquerors of Celtic in the first round. Their coach, a Hungarian, Geza Kalocsai, had already won one battle of tactics in the Soviet Union, precisely the place (a training-camp in temperate Georgia) where he took his players to beat the freeze in Poland. Gornik, a fast, intelligent side, included Stanislaw Oslizlo at centre-half, cool and indefatigable; Zygfryd Szoltysik, the hub of Gornik's dynamo; Hubert Kostka, a wonderful goalkeeper; and above all 'Wlodek' Lubanski, at twenty already among a handful of truly great forwards in Europe.

Gornik were clearly not match-fit when they came to Old Trafford, and it took a series of incredible saves from Kostka to keep them alive. Whatever the angle, whatever the distance, he seemed unbeatable—tipping over from Crerand, punching from Charlton, smothering from Best. Even Aston, striking the ball with the full meat of his boot from barely six yards, gaped disbelievingly when Kostka turned the shot away, quicker than the eye could see.

United's pressure, relentless and continuous, nevertheless exposed them to the swift counter-attacks that were Gornik's speciality. One matchless move between Szoltysik and Olek through the centre and down the left gave Lubanski a clear sight of goal and time to pick his spot; but he slightly miskicked and Stepney got down to the ball at the last possible moment. It was a chance that Lubanski, of all people, should not have missed.

In the second half Best showed just how expensive it was. Dunne reached Crerand, Crerand passed through no apparent gap to Best, who wriggled rapidly past two defenders, leaving the despairing Florenski to intercept only at the cost of kicking into his own goal. Even then United's progress was stalagmitic, and it seemed that Kostka would not be beaten for another light year. But in the very last minute Kidd found himself in possession at the extreme right of the penalty area and shot slowly, so slowly, on the diagonal to the far corner. The ball rolled remorselessly on, past one outstretched leg, then another, then a third, until it crept away from the unsighted Kostka and over the line. Kidd could not have chosen a better moment for an almost impossible goal, for threading the elephant through the eye of a needle.

Law had missed this match, suffering from an injury that was to plague him for the rest of the season. His knee, as Busby said, 'was swollen like a balloon'. Nor could he play in the return, which took place at Chorzow, halfway between Zabrze and the county town of Katowice. In spite of a raging blizzard nearly 100,000 turned out to see a dour struggle between a massed defence and spasmodic attack, which United lost and therefore won by the narrowest possible margin of one goal.

After losing astonishingly 3-1 at home to Chelsea, they

had had ten days rest for the tie, which proved a test of endurance in conditions that threatened skill with disaster. Best, trying little ballet steps in the snow, kept the pressure off his defence; but when Dunne was hurt, becoming almost a passenger with his left ankle strapped up, Gornik often threatened to score. Twenty minutes from the end Stepney dribbled the ball out to the edge of the penalty area before clearing it and the referee, who had sent United a warning at half-time that he would not allow such tactics, gave an indirect free-kick. With the whole team on the line Kuchta could not find a way through, but it so disorganised United's defence that a minute later his diagonal cross from the right reached Lubanski, whose furious shot scored off the underside of the crossbar. In former times, this might have been the signal for a general collapse; but with Stiles and Fitzpatrick everywhere, United made sure that their wall would not be breached again.

Law returned for United's momentous encounter with Real Madrid, their first meeting in Europe for eleven years, and a long-awaited opportunity for revenge. Charlton and Foulkes were United's only survivors; Gento similarly for Real, whom he now captained. With Law lacking the vital spark that could make him such a formidable opponent, United struggled hard to find a way through the mesh of Real's ironclad defence, linked in concentric circles by Gonzalez, Zunzunegui, Sanchis, Zoco and Luis. Their best chances fell in the opening minutes, when Betancort barely reached Aston's header from a Best cross, flinging himself full-length to hold the ball at the foot of the post. From the ensuing corner kick Crerand hit the post, but all to no avail. It took a fine run by Aston down and round the left perimeter, and an instant, explosive shot by Best from his short final pass to give United the lead. An hour remained, but United could not recreate such a rapier lunge, Sanchis subduing even Best with marvellous concentration and intensive marking. Just before the end, with Old Trafford at fever pitch, a glimmer of an opening came out of Crerand's interplay with Best and Charlton. But Kidd, not quite in tune with the orchestra, lifted his shot a few inches over the bar.

The lead seemed a precarious one to take to the cauldron of Chamartin, especially as Amancio, suspended after a sending-off in the previous round, would be back to add skill and dynamism to Real's attack. But Law was taken to Madrid only as a tactical manoeuvre: there was no chance of him playing, and shortly afterwards the cause of his mysterious injury, a small piece of broken bone lodged in his leg, condemned him to an operation.

United's form was ominously erratic: they had lost 6-3 (6-1 until near the end) at West Bromwich Albion, enabling Manchester City to creep above them on goal average. Even a 6-0 win over Newcastle did United no good; ironically, it merely softened up their opponents for a critical match with City the following week. With Leeds out of the race, United could only keep their title if they beat Sunderland at home and City lost at St James' Park. In the event, United suffered another home defeat and City won 4-3 in an exciting finale.

The championship, even if it had only crossed the city, was irretrievably lost: to stay in Europe United had to survive in Madrid. For half an hour they weathered the storm, but soon the firecrackers burst out from the towering terraces when Real seized a 3-1 lead to tilt the balance of the tie. As Amancio mocked United's defenders with his spectacular footwork, Stepney was left helpless and unsupported. First Amancio's bending free-kick soared to the head of Pirri, timing his leap and measuring the distance perfectly; then Brennan inexplicably missed Pirri's optimistic through pass and Gento was away, shooting ferociously through Stepney's legs as the goalkeeper made an unavailing advance. An unexpected present for United, Zoco slicing Dunne's lob past his own goalkeeper as Kidd challenged, seemed almost irrelevant; for immediately Amancio, crowded on the turn, somehow found the ingenuity to screw his shot past Stepney when no shot seemed possible.

At half-time, United were physically distressed and mentally defeated; but Busby picked them off the floor. Abandoning their massed defence, which had seemed fatally fallible, they gambled everything in attack, flinging Sadler upfield in support of the forwards. Real, feeling the match was already won, suddenly found it was slipping away in the last quarter of an hour. Crerand chipped a free-kick forward to the edge of the penalty area, Foulkes beat Zoco in the air, and the header curled innocuously towards goal. But Betancort left it to his defenders, the defenders left it to Betancort, and Sadler, seizing the golden opportunity, side-footed the ball on the volley past the stunned goalkeeper.

Level on aggregate, United summoned their reserves of strength for a final effort. There were twelve minutes left. Crerand, gripping the ball tightly, hurled a long throw up the right touchline, where Sanchis for once seemed too far removed from Best. Leaning against the tackle, Best took possession on the run, then, in a fantastic serpent-like motion, left Sanchis and Zoco groping at shadows. Free on the by-line he pushed the ball back for the tide of United attackers, and it was Foulkes, rolling back the years to Munich and before, who turned his deadly pass into the far corner. Soon came the end, and amidst deafening silence Busby embraced his players in a scene of tears and joy. By refusing to accept defeat, United had added a new, dramatic dimension to their morale, and won a chance to play at Wembley for the greatest prize of all.

13

The Teasing of Matt Busby

Wembley on European Cup Final day: a sea of waving hats and scarves, huge banners smuggled ingeniously past the police and officials, rattles and bugles in stereophonic competition. Above all, a sound—a cacophony that numbed the senses, swirling into a thunderous, throaty roar as the teams entered the arena. Conversation was abandoned or reduced to lip reading as the noise whirled around the head, like a hurricane condensed into a wind tunnel.

A single whistle that signalled the start of the match drowned the sound for Manchester United. It sunk into their subconscious, like the familiar rumble of a train in trackside houses. Their minds were on the match, a microcosm of sweat and stamina, with its own earth and sky.

Soon Aston, clad, with the rest of United, all in blue—the colours his father had worn in the Cup final twenty years before—tested Adolfo and found him wanting. He could beat the Portuguese back for speed, on the left and on the right, or for skill—cheekily, even, with a darting push between his bovine legs. Benfica were forced to move Humberto out of the middle to smother the inevitable run and cross from the wing.

Best had more room to work, but taunted too many

opponents, sacrificing teamwork for some individual vendetta. He was bruised and battered, tripped and harried by the relentless Cruz, who sensed the wrath of the referee and left the next foul to Humberto—predictably, Humberto's name went down in the little book.

All United's early effort seemed irrelevant when Eusebio brought down a stray pass twenty-five yards out, and let fly with a shot of such blinding force that Stepney gazed disbelievingly and made no effort to save. The ball dipped wickedly in flight, left the crossbar shuddering on its supports, and rebounded into play. Eusebio had almost made a goal out of nothing, from a position of apparent safety. He swung his arm in exasperation: the fifth time he had hit the woodwork at Wembley, with only one goal to show for it.

United slightly revised their strategy, challenging Eusebio at long range. Stiles played him as he had during the World Cup, preferring someone else to make the first tackle, so he could choose his moment for a crocodile snap while Eusebio was wriggling clear. Sometimes, when United so forgot themselves to allow four men upfield, Stiles was left frighteningly alone, forced to commit himself; he seemed infuriated when Eusebio tumbled theatrically, magnifying the foul—when there was no foul at all. So sure was Stiles on one occasion that he had been framed, that he did a little fall and feint to demonstrate Eusebio's bluff to the referee. Concetto lo Bello, the Sicilian police chief from Syracuse, continued to penalise Stiles for loitering with intent; but he must have been momentarily impressed, for Stiles' next and worst tackle of the night brought Eusebio down without punishment.

More free-kicks were awarded against Foulkes, who

made excessive use of Torres' shoulders in an effort to reduce the alarming gap between their heights in the air. Each time Eusebio paced out a run like a fast bowler trying to intimidate a suspect batsman, but United organised their defensive line with such fastidiousness, that usually he gave up the search for gaps. One fulminating shot did penetrate the wall, to an accompanying sound uncannily like crumbling mortar, but it slowed enough for Stepney to scramble the ball against his body.

The ruthless tackling and the jarring note of the referee's whistle reduced the first half to a staccato movement, art work with jagged ends. Benfica had come within inches of a score, but against this Sadler, put clean through by Kidd, missed horribly with the goal at his mercy. Henrique advanced, Sadler was in two minds whether to shoot or move the ball past him, and eventually stabbed beyond the far post with the crowd seething in frustration. Perhaps the strain of his schizophrenic role was too great, for Wembley is a long pitch, and Sadler ran up and down like a yo-yo.

Sadler, nevertheless, had a foot in United's opening goal that opened the game to a flashing array of chance and counter-chance. Dunne worked the ball down to him on the left, Charlton soared to his cross with more optimism than timing, and his header slid off his thinning hair into the far corner. Henrique, who had committed himself to an interception, was helpless to change a trajectory that left Charlton surprised but delighted. Benfica cast caution aside in an effort to equalise, turning Simoes and José Augusto back into orthodox wingers, flinging Coluna and the admirable Graca into a reckless offensive. Without them, Benfica's defence was precariously stretched, and after another run by Aston, Best cut them to ribbons, but Sadler's final shot hit Henrique's outstretched foot and bounced exasperatingly over the bar.

This was an expensive miss, which Benfica exploited to the full. Ten minutes from time Torres at last found Foulkes out of range, headed down carefully to Graca, who dashed in to score emphatically with a low cross shot from right to left. United visibly tottered at this reversal of fortune and Benfica sensed victory against the odds. Eusebio launched himself forward for a shot that Stepney stopped marvellously, low to his right. Then came the critical moment, the grain of sand that tilted the fine balance. When Graca found Eusebio again, he beat two defenders and this time kept going, like a matador delivering the killer thrust. Stepney was in an agony of doubt, came out too far and was moving backwards to avert a lob when Eusebio shot ferociously on the run from the edge of the penalty area. The ball was a blur, yet, quicker than the eye could see, Stepney twisted to his left and checked its flight. Afterwards he tried to play down his save, saying that 'the ball was within my reach, just to my left. To my amazement, I found the ball was softer than earlier in the match. If it had been as hard as at the start, it might have travelled faster and beaten me.' But Crerand thought the save was 'quite fantastic, certainly the turning point'. Eusebio was equally amazed: he ran up to Stepney after he had cleared the ball, shook his hand and applauded.

So United lived dangerously until the end of ordinary time. As Stiles said: 'If there had been another ten minutes Benfica would have won. We were shattered at the end of ninety minutes and collapsed on the turf. But when we looked around they were in a worse plight than us. They did not want to get up and start again, just like the Germans in the World Cup final.'

The teasing of Matthew Busby, who had gone through agonies on the trainer's bench, was over; now came the reward. In the first minute of extra time Stepney produced a long clearance which Kidd headed forward for Best. Cruz tried to intercept, but his legs lagged behind his thoughts, and Best was on the ball, sensing blood. Henrique came out expertly, Best swerved to his left on an extravagant diagonal, until for one sickening moment it seemed he would either catch his own pass too late or Henrique, diving backwards desperately, would make a dramatic stop on the line. But Best timed his final shot to the second, and although Henrique arrived at his intended objective, the ball was nestling in the back of the netting with Wembley repeating its Niagara roar.

Benfica reeled, and United came in for the kill. Charlton took a corner on the left which Kidd, on his nineteenth birthday, headed fiercely at Henrique. The goalkeeper flailed the ball away, but Kidd rose again like a jack-in-the-box, and his second header curled into the net from the underside of the crossbar. Now even United could hear the crowd, a torrent of noise, that re-echoed around the girders in an awe-inspiring crescendo. Kidd was still not finished. A run down the right, a precise pass to Charlton, whose dazzling flick curled beautifully into the far corner. The match was over, for although Eusebio brought another fine save out of Stepney, Benfica had already conceded defeat.

Busby left his team to their triumph, left Bobby Charlton to collect the European Cup, left Nobby Stiles to produce his famous toothless grin and do another jig of joy for a delirious Wembley. It was a moment of high emotion, a dream come true, a pinnacle of exultation after a valley of dark despair. It may not have been the greatest United team that took the trophy, but it had those priceless qualities of resilience and experience to do what no other Football League team had done.

As the new United paraded with the Cup, one sensed the gleeful, whispering shadows of the old, flitting across a field they had graced in the sunshine. Busby, a man of deep compassion and understanding, remains the magnet of them all. Replying to the question 'What makes a Manchester United footballer?' he said: 'I give you the answer in three words: skill, fitness, character, and the greatest of these is—character.'

Albert Quixall summed up the rare atmosphere at Old Trafford. 'In a way Matt is like a successful preacher. He makes you believe what he believes. His way of doing things becomes the only way of doing things. His mixture of personal humility and ruthless judgement is what makes the challenge of being a Manchester United player so exhilarating. You know you won't be judged by match results, but individually by mysterious standards buried deep inside Matt himself, and only him. He doesn't want merely a successful Manchester United. He wants the sort of team which will make everyone in Britain rejoice at his success.'

Matthew Busby has achieved his ambition: for Britain does rejoice.

INDEX